W9-CII-092

Holy Holy Land

Holy Holy Land

A DEVOTIONAL ANTHOLOGY

Edited by

Charles L. Wallis

Photographs by
Archie Lieberman

1817

HARPER & ROW, PUBLISHERS, NEW YORK, EVANSTON, AND LONDON

ACKNOWLEDGMENTS

Acknowledgment is made to the following for permission to reprint copyrighted material:

ABINGDON PRESS for "The Bread of Life" and "When Jesus Washed the Feet of Judas" from *More Hilltop Verses and Prayers* by Ralph S. Cushman, copyright 1949 by Pierce and Smith; "Jacob's Well" from *Holy Flame and Other Poems* by Georgia Harkness, copyright renewal 1963 by Georgia Harkness; "Prayer on Good Friday" from *The Glory of God* by Georgia Harkness, copyright 1943 by Whitmore and Stone; "Transfiguration" from *Be Still and Know* by Georgia Harkness, copyright renewal 1963 by Georgia Harkness; "The Law and the Beatitudes" from *In Green Pastures* by Janet Merchant, copyright © 1959 by Abingdon Press; "The Mount of the Beatitudes" from *Blessed Are You* by Jane Merchant, copyright © 1961 by Abingdon Press.

AMERICAN BIBLE SOCIETY for "Always a Star" by Gilbert Darlington from *Bible Society Record*.

AUGSBURG PUBLISHING HOUSE for extract from *Wonder in God's Wilderness* by Samuel J. Schmiechen, copyright © 1967 by Augsburg Publishing House.

BETHANY PRESS for "Temptation" from *Thy Sea So Great* by Winfred Ernest Garrison.

CHRISTIAN CENTURY FOUNDATION for "Condemnation" by Sara King Carleton; "Gloria in Excelsis" by Donald J. Cunningham; "As Peter Loved" by Jean Hogan Dudley; "The First Friends' Meeting" by I. Sutherland Groom; "Galilee" by Wilson MacDonald; "The Young Messiah" by Leslie Clare Manchester.

CHURCH OF SCOTLAND COMMITTEE ON THE RELIGIOUS INSTRUCTION OF YOUTH for extract from *The Life and Teaching of Jesus Christ* by James S. Stewart.

DOUBLEDAY AND COMPANY, INC., for extract from *Peace with God* by Billy Graham, copyright 1953 by Billy Graham.

WILLIAM B. EERDMANS PUBLISHING COMPANY for extracts from *Feeling Low?, Reflections,* and *Thoughts Afield* by Harold E. Kohn.

THE FREE METHODIST for "Hidden Light" by Ethel G. Bemis.

FRIENDSHIP PRESS for extract from *Edge of the Edge* by Theodore E. Matson.

HARPER & ROW, PUBLISHERS, INC., for extract from *The Geography of the Bible* by Denis Baly; extracts from *Deliverance to the Captives* by Karl Barth; extract from *God's Turn* by Henry Sloane Coffin; "His Garment's Hem," "Jesus Was a Poet," "Thirty-Three Years," and "The White Fire of Beauty" from *Poems of Inspiration and Courage* by Grace Noll Crowell; extract from *The Modern Use of the Bible* by Harry Emerson Fosdick; "Fishers" by Albert Reginald Gold from *At Worship*; "The Carpenter" by Phyllis Hartnoll from *Christ and the Fine Arts*; extract from *Creative Prayer* by Emily Herman; extract from *A Testament of Devotion* by Thomas R. Kelly; extract from *Anno Domini* by Kenneth Scott Latourette; extract from *The Hand of God* by Oswald W. S. McCall; "The Day and the Work," "The Place

of Peace," and "We Have Broken Our Bread Together" from *Poems of Edwin Markham*; extract from *Jesus, Man of Genius* by John Middleton Murry; extract from *That They May Have Life* by Daniel T. Niles; "Song" by Charles G. Blanden and "Strength" by Jessie Wilmore Murton from *One Thousand Quotable Poems*; "Paul" from *Selected Poems of John Oxenham*; "Carpenter Christ" by Mildred Fowler Field, "Apocalypse" by Ruth Frost, "Peace" by Jessie Rose Gates, and "A Singing Heart" by Winnie Lynch Rockett from *Poems for Life*; "Barabbas Speaks," "I Who Love Beauty," and "Two Chalices" from *Over the Sea, the Sky* by Edwin McNeill Poteat; extract from *On Beginning from Within* by Douglas V. Steere; extract from *Asking for Trouble* by Bruno Scott James; "The Prayer of the Quest" by Eleanor B. Stock from *Masterpieces of Religious Verse*; "Work" from *The Unutterable Beauty* by G. A. Studdert-Kennedy; extract from *The Bridge of San Luis Rey* by Thornton Wilder.

HYMN SOCIETY OF AMERICA for "Above the Hills of Time" and "When the Daylight Wanes" by Thomas Tiplady.

HOLT, RINEHART AND WINSTON, INC., for "The Parting" and "The Path of the Stars" from *Shadow of the Perfect Rose* by Thomas S. Jones, Jr., copyright 1937, © 1965 by John L. Foley.

P.E.O. RECORD for "The Lamp of Love" by Mary

Aldrich Beechner; "Be Glad for Living" by Mildred Tatlock Binder; "Benediction" by Wilda English; "Life Gave Me These" by Zella G. Wallace; and "Nothing New" by Betty L. Whitsell.

PULPIT DIGEST for prayer by William Robert Miller, copyright © 1958 by The Pulpit Digest Publishing Company.

FLEMING H. REVELL COMPANY for extract from *When Christmas Came to Bethlehem* by Charles L. Allen and Charles L. Wallis.

SIGNS OF THE TIMES for "A Prayer" by Maryan B. Wilkinson.

SIMON & SCHUSTER, INC., for extract from *The New Book of the Art of Living* by Wilferd A. Peterson, copyright © 1962, 1963 by Wilferd A. Peterson.

SPIRIT MAGAZINE for "Meditation on Jesus Christ" by Johanna Rachel Branigan.

SUNSHINE MAGAZINE for quotations by E. C. Baird, Leo Bennett, Edgar Frank, F. A. Hornibrook, and Kirby Page; "Miracles" by Frances E. Walker.

UPPER ROOM for "Meditation for Holy Communion" by Russell Q. Chilcote, copyright 1954 by The Upper Room.

UNITED CHURCH PRESS for "Housewife," "Simon," and "Simple Faith" from *Tribute to Jesus* by Edgar Daniel Kramer.

WESTMINSTER PRESS for "Put Yourself into the Path of the Wind" by Myra Scovel from *Today*, copyright 1957 by The Westminster Press.

(See additional acknowledgments on page 218.)

HOLY HOLY LAND. Copyright © 1969 by Charles L. Wallis.

Photographs copyright © 1969 by Archie Lieberman.

Printed in the United States of America. All rights reserved.

For information address

Harper & Row, Publishers, Incorporated,

49 East 33rd Street, New York, N.Y. 10016.

FIRST EDITION

LIBRARY OF CONGRESS CATALOG CARD NUMBER: 79-85046

CONTENTS

Inscribed to
MELVIN L. ARNOLD

❖❖❖

PREFACE

Blest land of Judea! thrice hallowed of
    song;
Where the holiest of memories pilgrim-like
    throng;
In the shade of thy palms, by the shores
    of thy sea,
On the hills of thy beauty, my heart is
    with thee.

Blue sea of the hills! in my spirit I hear
Thy waters, Gennesaret, chime on my ear;
Where the lowly and just with the people
    sat down,
And thy spray on the dust of His sandals
    was thrown.

O here with His flock the sad Wanderer
    came;
These hills He toiled over in grief are
    the same;
The founts where He drank by the way-
    side still flow,
And the same airs are blowing which
    breathed on His brow.

          JOHN GREENLEAF WHITTIER

❖❖❖

Forty centuries ago Abraham left the Baby-
lonian city of Ur and journeyed into the
Holy Land. He and his children were
blessed by God, and that blessing sustains
us to this day.

By faith Abraham "looked for a city
which hath foundations, whose builder and
maker is God" (Heb. 11:10). God's covenant with Abraham, confirmed in Jesus
Christ and renewed in the life and testimony of Christians, guides us in our pilgrimage toward that "house not made with
hands, eternal in the heavens" (II Cor. 5:1).

In the Holy Land are the spiritual landmarks of the heart and shrines of the
soul. The soil and waters of the Promised
Land are sacred to countless multitudes,
for from this ageless country have come
abiding convictions of the human race,
the gift of law and ritual, the clarion ring
of prophets' voices, and the Holy Scriptures which are a lamp unto our feet and
a light unto our path.

In Palestine the Son of God was born.
Here He grew to manhood, ministered to
the sick in body and mind, taught imperishable truths, offered His life in love
upon a cross, arose triumphant from the
grave, and bequeathed to all who trust
Him a legacy of saving grace.

This book is a devotional guide in word
and picture of those scenes hallowed by
the footsteps and living words of Jesus
Christ. Herein we look "unto the rock
whence ye are hewn" (Isa. 51:1). "That
Rock was Christ" is the ringing affirmation
of the Apostle Paul.

These pages are more than a sentimental
journey into the past. They offer medita-
tions for our renewal and confidence as
we look forward in faith and hope.

          CHARLES L. WALLIS

Keuka College
Keuka Park, New York

Galilee

. . . in Him was life

LIFE

❖❖❖

SCRIPTURE

Jesus came into Galilee, preaching the gospel of the kingdom of God, and saying, The time is fulfilled, and the kingdom of God is at hand: repent ye, and believe the gospel. Now as he walked by the sea of Galilee, he saw Simon and Andrew his brother casting a net into the sea: for they were fishers. And Jesus said unto them, Come ye after me, and I will make you to become fishers of men.

MARK 1:14–17

And Jesus . . . came nigh unto the sea of Galilee; and went up into a mountain, and sat down there. And great multitudes came unto him, having with them those that were lame, blind, dumb, maimed, and many others, and cast them down at Jesus' feet; and he healed them: insomuch that the multitude wondered, when they saw the dumb to speak, the maimed to be whole, the lame to walk, and the blind to see: and they glorified the God of Israel.

MATTHEW 15:29–31

I am come that they might have life, and that they might have it more abundantly.

JOHN 10:10

❖❖❖

MEDITATION

Holy, holy, holy, Lord, Thy disciples
Gather in devotion, to sing and dream
  of Thee:
Holy, holy, holy, beautiful and gracious,
Still in our hearts we dwell in Galilee.

These words of Percy MacKaye mirror the abiding hold with which Galilee clings to the hearts of all Christians. For it was in this northern portion of Palestine that Jesus spent most of His incarnate life. He knew well the sixty-odd villages and cities in this land of hills and fertile valleys. He walked the shores of the blue-sweet waters of the Sea of Galilee.

Here first in Nazareth and later in Capernaum He lived. Here He was baptized. Here He called from among the simple-mannered and intensely religious people those who formed the inner circle of love and discipleship. Here He performed the first and many of the most memorable of His miracles. Here He gave to humanity the deathless words of His Sermon on the Mount. Here, we read, the people "heard him gladly." Here was situated the Mount of Transfiguration. And here, the Elder John tells us, will be the scene of Armageddon.

As the caravan roads crossing Galilee led to the far-ranging centers of world population, so the words of Jesus, carried on the mystic wings of the Spirit, have gone to the uttermost ends of the earth.

9

MEMORY AND HOPE

The Christian faith is a blending of memory and hope.

But the memory is such as to provide incentive and daring for the needs of today.

And the hope has no validity except as it is grounded in the brave and faithful performance of contemporary responsibilities.

TRUMAN B. DOUGLASS

THE FIRST FRIENDS' MEETING

Anno Domini 34
Mary and Lazarus sat in sycamore shade
    silent as love:
wrapped in a calm that formed no barricade the while they strove
to live again
those Bethany hours when Jesus walked
    with men.

No speech, no touch communion, there
    they stayed, their darkened eyes
striving to visualize Him, there they essayed to realize
the peace He shed;
till Martha came to meet them, bringing
    bread.

I. SUTHERLAND GROOM

A NEW BEGINNING

Jesus gave history a new beginning. In every land He is at home. Everywhere men think His face is like their best face—and like God's face. His birthday is kept across the world. His death-day has set a gallows against every city skyline.

GEORGE A. BUTTRICK

THE BLESSING OF THE DEW

Palestine lived by its dews almost as much as by its rains.

Moisture-laden winds drenched the cool nights with dew and kept the pastures alive, as though each grass blade made its own cloud and welcomed the dawn with jeweled drops.

Life, said the sad poet-prophet, is like that.

When the greater blessings are withheld we must learn to live by the lesser mercies —and they will not fail us.

Indeed the greatest blessings reach us only in intimate ways.

Love comes to our hearts from our hearthstones.

Duty is the succession of daily tasks.

Happiness is the well-being of the near and the dear.

Like the dew of Palestinian hills, the ocean of God's providence comes to us in such ways as even a grass blade can take and grow by.

GAIUS GLENN ATKINS

THE DOORS OF HEAVEN

In silver light of dawn the children wait
With poet mystics at the eastern gate.
Warmhearted people stand with joy before
The glowing splendor of the southern
    door.
In cool, clear noonday thoughtful throngs
    attest
The thinkers find the northern portal best.
And on the west, at sunset of the day,
The doors take the rugged western way.

GAIL BROOK BURKET

MANIFESTATION

Our lives are a manifestation of what we think about God.

CHRISTIAN HERALD

THE PATHWAYS OF
THE HOLY LAND

The pathways of Thy land are little
    changed
  Since Thou wert there:
The busy world through other ways has
    ranged,
  And left these bare.

The rocky path still climbs the glowing
    steep
  Of Olivet,
Though rains of two millenniums wear it
    deep,
  Men tread it yet.

Still to the gardens o'er the brook it leads,
  Quiet and low;
Before his sheep the shepherd on it treads,
  His voice they know.

The wild fig throws broad shadows o'er it
    still,
  As once o'er Thee;
Peasants go home at evening up that hill
  To Bethany.

And as when gazing Thou didst weep o'er
    them,
  From height to height
The white roofs of discrowned Jerusalem
  Burst on our sight.

These ways were strewn with garments
    once, and palm,
  Which we tread thus;
Here through Thy triumph on Thou
    passedst, calm,
  On to Thy cross.

The waves have washed fresh sands upon
    the shore,
  Of Galilee;
But chiselled in the hillsides evermore
  Thy paths we see.

Man has not changed them in that slum-
    bering land,

Nor time effaced:
Where Thy feet trod to bless we still may
    stand;
  All can be traced.

Yet we have traces of Thy footsteps far
  Truer than these;
Where'er the poor and tired and suffering
    are,
  Thy steps faith sees.

Nor with fond sad regrets Thy steps we
    trace;
  Thou art not dead!
Our path is onward, till we see Thy face,
  And hear Thy tread.

And now, wherever meets Thy lowliest
    band
  In praise and prayer,
There is Thy presence, there Thy Holy
    Land,
  Thou, Thou art there!

ELIZABETH RUNDLE CHARLES

❖❖❖

Christ came not to talk about a beautiful
light, but to be that light, not to speculate
about virtue, but to be virtue.

H. G. TAYLOR

❖❖❖

THE PRESENCE OF GOD

The presence of God has no relation to
this place or that. Whatever duty or devotion calls, we shall find God at hand.

If we are right with Him, we may be just
as conscious and just as sure of His presence in the little cottage kitchen as in a
great assembly of the saints.

His presence is to be realized as truly at
the bottom of a coalpit as in a sunny forest
glade.

The place is nothing to Him. The person He comes to meet and live with is
everything.

BRAMWELL BOOTH

NEW DISCLOSURE

I am very sure that the first outpouring of New Testament happiness—the thing which, rising like a flood, caught in its mighty volume some simple men and made them great—was not this or that in the man Jesus, however tender and rebuking, but some new disclosure—incredible until accepted, whereupon it became almost too much for the human heart, too astonishing and good—some new disclosure of the nature and disposition of God. The glory of Jesus to those who first loved Him and gave themselves for Him, was that He was the answer from God to those questions as to our significance in this world, as to the value of any high behavior, as to whether life in the long run and all the way leads on to a contradiction, or leads on to God.

JOHN A. HUTTON

LIFELINE

A true follower of Jesus will use a map which includes the whole world and all the people in it.

BRUCE R. BAXTER

FISHERS

Tangled in nets
    Of our wild philosophy,
Caught in the backlash
    Of ideas ill-cast,
Heaving the lead
    Into unplumbed infinity,
Baffled we stand
    Beside the shore at last,
Snagged barbs, snarled lines,
    Torn sails! What fishers we!
Teach us Thy skill,
    O Man of Galilee.

ALBERT REGINALD GOLD

IN PALESTINE

Have the rocks on the hillside voices—
    And the clods under trampling feet?
Do the cobblestones utter a message?
    And the pebbles tell secrets sweet?

Yes, the hills and the vales have voices,
    The rocks by the wayside speak:
They tell of the march of the ages,
    And of Him whom the nations seek.

GEORGE W. CARLIN

PURPOSE

The purpose of life is not to be happy—but to matter, to be productive, to be useful, to have it make some difference that you lived at all.

LEO ROSTEN

THE HILLS KEEP HOLY GROUND

When morning moves in slow processional
    To worship day, the hills keep holy
        ground,
Where spirit meets in high confessional
    The presence of Infinity, and sound
Of an eternal power stirs the air.
    From silence unto silence echoes roll
The deep acclaim of consciousness aware
    Of oneness with the universal soul.

No prophet blessed the quiet of these hills,
    Nor stood at prayer before their solitude.
But in their boundless peace of mind fulfills
    Diameters of vision that include
Eternity, the instant of God's hand—
    Who worships here has found the Holy
        Land.

HELLENE SEAMAN

12

THE MANLINESS OF CHRIST

The real truth about the manliness of
Christ seems to be this: that He is so like
us that He makes us know that we may
be like Him, and so unlike us that He
makes us know that we must be unlike
our present selves before we can be like
Him. His life fits in among our human
lives like a jewel which is so adapted to
the gold into which it is set that nobody
can doubt that they are made for one
another, and yet which so far fails of
suiting its place perfectly that we can see
that the gold has been bent and twisted
and must be twisted back again in order
to accommodate it perfectly. He is at once
our satisfaction and our rebuke. He has
our human qualities; He feels our human
motives; but in Him they take new shapes.
It is with Him as it is with our best and
noblest friends. They all first claim us by
their likeness, and then shame and instruct
us by their unlikeness. So it is with the
manliness of Jesus.

PHILLIPS BROOKS

❖❖❖

Does the Christian need life?
   Jesus Christ is his life.
Does he seek wisdom?
   In Jesus Christ are "stored up all the
      treasures of wisdom and knowledge."
Does he long for righteousness?
   Christ has been made "our righteous-
      ness."
Does his soul hunger?
   Jesus Christ is the "true bread."
Is his spirit barren, arid?
   Jesus Christ is unto him a "fountain of
      living water."

RICHARD C. HALVERSON

LO, I AM WITH YOU ALWAYS

Wide fields of corn along the valley spread;
   The rain and dews mature the swelling
      vine;
I see the Lord in multiplying bread;
   I see Him turning water into wine;
I see Him working all the works divine
   He wrought when Salemward His steps
      were led;
The selfsame miracles around Him shine;
   He feeds the famished; He revives the
      dead;
He pours the flood of light on darkened
      eyes;
   He chases tears, diseases, fiends away;
His throne is raised upon these orient
      skies;
   His footstool is the pave whereon we
      pray.
Ah, tell me not of Christ in Paradise,
   For He is all around us here today.

JOHN CHARLES EARLE

❖❖❖

BE GLAD FOR LIVING

Be glad for living! Do not see your day
As strings of hours heavy with demands;
Accept their challenge with a steadfast
      faith
God will not overburden willing hands.

Accept your duties with the self-respect
Of feeling He has chosen only you
To do them, and your glory in each task
Will bring a recompense forever new!

MILDRED TATLOCK BINDER

❖❖❖

And His that gentle voice we hear,
Soft as the breath of even,
That checks each fault, that calms each
      fear,
And speaks of heaven.

HARRIET AUBER

❖❖❖

❖❖❖

The supreme miracle of Christ's character lies in this: that He combines within Himself, as no other figure in human history has ever done, the qualities of every race. His very birthplace and home in childhood were near the concourse of the two great streams of human life in the ancient world that flowed East and West. Time and place conspired, but the divine spark came down from above to mould for all time the human character of the Christ, the Son of Man.

CHARLES F. ANDREWS

❖❖❖

PAUL'S AMBITION

Paul lived in the atmosphere of religion every hour of the day. No portrait of him is complete which ignores his life in God.

In God he lived and moved and had his being, not unconsciously as with most of us, but consciously.

He was sure of God, sure of His existence, sure of His active participation in human affairs in general, and in Paul's affairs in particular.

God guided him day by day. Because he is religious, he loves to pray. He is always speaking with God. His prayerfulness is one of the most conspicuous features of his character.

There is nothing more certain in the whole history of the Christian Church than that the greatest of the apostles was a man who spent much time in communion with God.

To be like God was Paul's supreme ambition. He wants to partake of the divine nature. His burning desire is to become a man full statured in God's sight.

Paul came to know God in a new way through Christ, and therefore Paul's theology is a Christology.

The central word in his vocabulary is "Christ." God is in Christ reconciling the world to Himself. Christ is the image of the invisible God. In Christ there dwells all the fullness of the godhead.

If God is in Christ, then the death of Christ is not a sign of failure but of triumph. It seems weakness but it is the power of God. It appears to be foolishness, but it is the wisdom of God.

It is by the Cross of Christ that God is going to save the world.

CHARLES E. JEFFERSON

❖❖❖

CRUCIFIXION

He sang, too,
    In the lanes of Nazareth,
With sunlit eyes, and boyish voice
    Quickly out of breath.

He dreamed, too,
    Of mountains and a city,
Where men would trample gems
    And treasure pity.

He loved, too,
    But someway friends forgot,
When swords and staves and kisses
    Cut the lover's knot.

He grieved, too,
    For all His songs unsung.
They gave Him vinegar for songs
    Upon a parching tongue.

He sighed, too,
    With quickly failing breath,
For souls and songs and little lanes
    In Nazareth.

EARL MARLATT

❖❖❖

Christian worship is the most momentous,
the most urgent,
the most glorious action
that can take place in human life.

KARL BARTH

15

JESUS OF NAZARETH PASSETH BY

Watcher, who watch'st by the bed of pain,
  While the stars sweep on in their mid-
    night train;
Stifling the tear for thy loved one's sake;
  Holding thy breath, lest his sleep should
    break;
In the loneliest hours, there is a helper
    nigh,
  "Jesus of Nazareth passeth by."

Stranger, afar from thy native land,
  Whom no one takes with a brother's
    hand,
Table, and hearthstone are glowing free,
  Casements are sparkling, but not for
    thee,
There is one who can tell of a home on
    high,
  "Jesus of Nazareth passeth by."

Sad one, in secret, bending low,
  A dart in thy breast, that the world may
    not know.
Striving the favor of God to win,—
  Asking His pardon for days of sin;
Press on, press on, with thy earnest cry,
  "Jesus of Nazareth passeth by."

Mourner, who sits in the church-yard lone,
  Scanning the lines on that marble
    stone,—
Plucking the weeds from thy children's
    bed,
  Planting the myrtle, the rose instead—
Look up, look up, with thy tearful eye,
  "Jesus of Nazareth passeth by."

Fading one, with the hectic streak,
  With thy vein of fire, and thy burning
    cheek,
Fear'st thou to tread the darkened vale?
  Look unto One, who can never fail.
He hath trod it Himself, He will hear thy
    sigh,
  "Jesus of Nazareth passeth by."

LYDIA H. SIGOURNEY

SHARED LIFE

In praying to God we are praying to Him whose life we share as we pray, and whose life is shared not by us alone but by those for whom we pray.

We do seem to have found the medium through which we may influence them aright—and that medium is God Himself.

As we make our prayer in the power of the spirit, "in the name of Christ," that same spirit is quickened in the spirit of those we love and pray for, for "we are all members of one body," and when "one member is glorified all the members rejoice with it."

LEONARD HODGSON

OCCUPATION

To occupy oneself with God is not to be idle. It is the one occupation of all occupations.

ST. BERNARD

COMPANIONSHIP

We do not only go with Christ. We meet Christ in those to whom we go.

MAX WARREN

THE HALLOWED LIFE

If you explore the life of things and of conditioned being, you come to the un-fathomable.

If you deny the life of things and of conditioned being, you stand before noth-ingness.

If you hallow this life, you meet the living God.

MARTIN BUBER

Nazareth

. . . the blessings of home

HOME

❖❖❖

An angel of the Lord appeareth in a dream to Joseph . . ., saying, Arise, and take the young child and his mother, and go into the land of Israel. . . . And he came and dwelt in a city called Nazareth: that it might be fulfilled which was spoken by the prophets, He shall be called a Nazarene.

MATTHEW 2:19–20, 23

And when he was twelve years old, they went up to Jerusalem after the custom of the feast. And when they had fulfilled the days. . . . he went down with them, and came to Nazareth, and was subject unto them. . . . And Jesus increased in wisdom and stature, and in favour with God and man.

LUKE 2:42–43, 51–52

And he came to Nazareth, where he had been brought up: and, as his custom was, he went into the synagogue on the sabbath day, and stood up for to read.

LUKE 4:16

Nathanael said unto him, Can there any good thing come out of Nazareth? Philip saith unto him, Come and see.

JOHN 1:46

❖❖❖

MEDITATION

Located in lower Galilee and more than eighty miles from the city of Jerusalem, Nazareth has only one claim on history. This was the place where Jesus grew to manhood. As such, Nazareth symbolizes for all Christians those gracious and good qualities which we attach to God-fearing home life.

Little is recorded regarding the childhood of Him who, more than all others, has bestowed a sacramental character upon family relations. Yet we know that from Joseph and His mother Mary, who were responsive to God's will for their lives, the Boy learned the matchless lessons of life which, through His teachings, would later pass on to par-

ents for twenty succeeding centuries.

What were those imperishable lessons? That God is a loving Father. That all men are His children. That every human being is called into the household of God. That beyond present circumstances is a heavenly house of many mansions to which the eternal Father invites His loved ones.

From the heights above Nazareth the Boy Jesus looked many times upon a picturesque panorama including Mount Carmel and the Plain of Esdraelon. But His vision encompassed much more. Beyond the horizon He discerned a family of mankind bound to God by devotion, loyalty, and commitment.

❖❖❖

JESUS AT HOME

Nazareth stands for the home life. It contains the greater part of His great career. By far the greater number of years was spent here.

Here were more praying for others and over the life plan, more communing with the Father, more battling with temptation and narrow prejudice and ignorance than in the few years of public service.

Here were more purity of life and steadiness of purpose, more wisdom in action and patience in touch with others and with the knotty little problems of daily life, more of all this being lived than could ever find outlet at His lips.

Those three years and odd of public life all grew out of this Nazareth home life. They are the top of the hill; Nazareth is the base and bulk; Calvary the tip-top where every victory had already been won.

The public life was built on home life. Under the ministering to crowds, healing the sick, raising the dead, and patient teaching of the multitudes, lay the great strong home life in its purity.

Calvary was built on Nazareth.

S. D. GORDON

❖❖❖

THE BOY JESUS

Once, measuring His height, He stood
    Beneath a cypress tree,
And, leaning back against the wood,
    Stretched wide His arms for me;
Whereat a brooding mother-dove
    Fled fluttering from her nest above.

At evening He loved to walk
    Among the shadowy hills and talk
Of Bethlehem;
    But if perchance there passed us by
The paschal lambs, He'd look at them
    In silence, long and tenderly;

And when again He'd try to speak,
I've seen the tears upon His cheek.

JOHN BANISTER TABB

❖❖❖

PRAYER

O Thou Christ of Galilee, who didst go into the homes and the hearts of many folk and kindle there a light which has burned through all the centuries: make each of us a humble sharer of Thy glory and goodness, so that we may find a purpose and meaning in life. Teach us to speak and act so that we may cheer and help men. Grant us love for all, that we may everywhere see Thy children and heed their cries.

FLOYD TOMPKINS

❖❖❖

THE HIDDEN YEARS

The hidden years at Nazareth!
    How deep and still they seem,
Like rivers flowing in the dark
    Or waters in a dream!
Like waters under Syrian stars
    Reflecting lights above,
Repeating in their silent depths
    The wonder of God's love!

The hidden years at Nazareth!
    How clear and true they lie,
As open to the smile of God
    As to the Syrian sky!
As open to the heart of man
    As to the genial sun,
With dreams of vast adventuring,
    And deeds of kindness done!

The hidden years of Nazareth!
    How radiant they rise,
With life and death in balance laid
    Before a Lad's clear eyes!
O Soul of Youth, forever choose,
    Forgetting fate or fear,
To live for truth or die with God,
    Who stands beside Thee here!

ALLEN EASTMAN CROSS

DEDICATION

O Thou whose gracious presence blest
    The home at Bethany,
This shelter from the world's unrest,
This home made ready for its Guest,
    We dedicate to Thee.

We build an altar here, and pray
    That Thou wilt show Thy face.
Dear Lord, if Thou wilt come to stay,
This home we consecrate today
    Will be a holy place.

LOUIS F. BENSON

❖❖❖

The Christian home is the Master's workshop where the processes of character molding are silently, lovingly, faithfully, and successfully carried on.

RICHARD MONCKTON MILNES

❖❖❖

AFTER CALVARY

For Martha, there were dishes
    To be washed ere close of day,
Matzoths to bake for breakfast,
    And crumbs to sweep away.
For Martha, there was dust-fluff,
    The board to set; a broom—
That kept her mind away from
    One hanging in the gloom.

For Mary, there was twilight
    And one star that kissed a hill;
For her were trees and springtime
    Beyond her windowsill.
For Mary, there were shadows,
    A lily's breath, a leaf—
That tore her heart with pity
    And nailed her soul with grief.

VIOLET ALLEYN STOREY

❖❖❖

MOTHERS OF THE BIBLE

Did you ever notice the way in which the Bible honors the mothers of men? They are placed in a hall of fame all their own. No matter whether he was a wise or a foolish, a righteous or an evil king, his mother's name is set down.

It all runs something like this. His mother's name was Jochebed. His mother's name was Jehoaddan. His mother's name was Zibiah. His mother's name was Jecholiah. His mother's name was Jerusha. His mother's name was Abi. His mother's name was Haphzibah. His mother's name was Hamutal. His mother's name was Jedidah. His mother's name was Micaiah. His mother's name was Elizabeth. His mother's name was Mary.

You will remember that it was a mother who said, "Grant that these my two sons may sit, the one on thy right hand, and the other on the left in thy kingdom." It is always so. Who else but a mother has a right to demand that her children shall sit on thrones and be wreathed with crowns? It is also important for us to remember that Jesus did not deny the plea, but promised to grant the request if her children would prove worthy.

Sometimes a mother's prayers fail, not because of what she has been or done, but because of the unworthiness of those who refuse the crown with which their mother would crown them.

HUGH THOMSON KERR

❖❖❖

SON OF MAN

He often spoke of things of home,
    Of linen white as snow,
Of platters cleansed inside and out,
    Of leaven hid in dough,
And lost coin sought with broom and lamp.
    Was He wistful, He
Who walked, alone, the road toward death,
    Homeless in Galilee?

LESLIE SAVAGE CLARK

❖❖❖

MY HOME
(Paraphrase of I Corinthians 13)

My home may be made beautiful by the wealth of the world, but if it has not love, it is only an empty shell.

My home may be the rendezvous of the witty and the meeting place of the wise, but if it has not love, it is only a noisy house.

My home may distribute its welcome to men of every estate, my home may toil for the betterment of all mankind, but if it has not love, its influence will soon vanish.

The spirit of a true home is very patient, very kind, it knows no jealousy, makes no parade, gives itself no airs, is never rude, never selfish, never irritated, never resentful.

It is never gladdened when sorrow comes to another home, is made happy by goodness, always slow to talk with others about the intimacies of the home, always eager to believe the best, always hopeful, always enduring.

The home will never disappear. As for civilizations, they will be superseded; as for knowledge, it will grow out of date; as for institutions, they will cease.

For we only know a little now and we can see only dimly into the future, but when the spirit of a true home rules the affairs of this earth, then will be established the perfect Kingdom of God.

Thus faith and hope and love last on forever in our homes, these three, but the greatest of all is love.

ROBERT W. BURNS

❖❖❖

Children are God's apostles sent forth, day by day, to preach of love and hope and peace.

JAMES RUSSELL LOWELL

❖❖❖

THE HOLY WOMEN

I have seen Mary at the Cross
    And Mary at the tomb
And Mary weeping as she spread her hair
    In a leper's room.

But it was not in Bethany
    Or groping up Calvary hill
I learned how women break their hearts
        to ease
    Another's ill.

Compassionate and wise in pain,
    Most faithful in defeat,
The holy Marys I have watched and loved
    Live on our street.

WILLIAM ALEXANDER PERCY

❖❖❖

YOUR CHILDREN'S GOD
AND THEIR HOME

How much have your children found in their home to make God real to them?

The sacrament might appeal to them more powerfully had every meal at home been given a sacramental flavor through the saying of grace.

The Bible might mean more to them had its great words and thoughts been interwoven with the home life.

Prayer might seem natural to them had they found it a part of the atmosphere of the home.

What does it mean when God says to your son or your daughter, who stands dazed, exalted, yet bewildered before this burning bush of modern knowledge, wondering vaguely what it means at the heart of it, "I am the God of your father and your mother"?

Does it open their eyes to the deep meaning of life? Or does it lead them to set religion aside with other childish things?

WILLIAM P. MERRILL

So sweetly through that humble home
 The rippling laughter went
That Mary felt the world's blue dome
 Too small for her content.

And careful Joseph, while he held
 The Boy in grave caress,
Wist not what tender thrill dispelled
 His workday weariness.

The crown set softly, only rings
 Of baby hair agleam
With lustres dropt from angel's wings
 And starlight down a dream.

The thorn-tree was a seedling still
 And with laughter's frolic chime
The Christ-child did His father's will,
 As when, of elder time,

A ruddy lad in Bethlehem
 Was keeping sheep and played
Blithe music on his harp to them
 Before the psalms were made.

KATHARINE LEE BATES

❖❖❖

HOME ATMOSPHERE

Homes at any time—ancient, modern, or ultra-tomorrow—depend upon the kind of persons who live in them. Joyous, creative persons who like living and more or less know what it's all about—they make happy, comfortable homes.

Defeated, morose persons hang a pall, like soiled drawn curtains, over their walls and windows. One cantankerous individual in a group of otherwise well-adjusted personalities can mighty nigh ruin a home.

But, on the other hand, one valiant spirit can redeem a whole household of mental misfits and spiritual dimwits. It's like that.

The atmosphere of a home is contagious.

In a home people depend upon one another closely. Also they depend upon things and their attitude toward things.

Ponderables, such as beds and pianos and silverware, and imponderables, such as fear of the grocery bill and pride of a window box, are all mixed in together in a home.

Which brings us back again to the fundamental fact that homes depend for their success or failure, for their quality and durability, upon persons.

MARGUERITTE HARMON BRO

❖❖❖

A LIVING EPISTLE

I heard about God from a preacher,
I read about God in His Word,
I learned about God from my Mother
Who was like all I read and heard.

MARY FOOT GRIFFING

❖❖❖

CHRISTMAS

A Boy was born at Bethlehem
 That knew the haunts of Galilee,
He wandered on Mount Lebanon,
 And learned to love each forest tree.

But I was born at Marlborough,
 And love the homely faces there;
And for all other men besides
 'Tis little love I have to spare.

I should not mind to die for them,
 My own dear owns, my comrades true.
But that great heart of Bethlehem
 He died for men He never knew.

And yet, I think, at Golgotha,
 As Jesus' eyes were closed in death,
They saw with love most passionate
 The village street at Nazareth.

E. HILTON YOUNG

Bethany

. . . the greatest of these is love

LOVE

✦✦✦

Being in Bethany in the house of Simon the leper, as he sat at meat, there came a woman having an alabaster box of ointment of spikenard very precious; and she brake the box, and poured it on his head. . . . And Jesus said . . . she hath wrought a good work on me.

MARK 14:3, 6

Now a certain man was sick, named Lazarus, of Bethany, the town of Mary and her sister Martha. . . . Therefore his sisters sent unto him, saying, Lord, behold, he whom thou lovest is sick. . . . Then when Jesus came, he found that he had lain in the grave four days already. . . . When Mary was come where Jesus was, and saw him, she fell down at his feet, saying unto him, Lord, if thou hadst been here, my brother had not died. . . . He cried with a loud voice, Lazarus, come forth. And he that was dead came forth.

JOHN 11:1, 3, 17, 32, 43–44

And he led them out as far as to Bethany, and he lifted up his hands, and blessed them. And it came to pass, while he blessed them, he was parted from them, and carried up into heaven.

LUKE 24:50–51

✦✦✦

MEDITATION

On the eastern slope of the Mount of Olives, two miles from Jerusalem, lay Bethany, the home of Jesus' beloved friends, Lazarus and his sisters, Mary and Martha.

These friends were surely among those who assembled near Bethany for the spontaneous procession which we recall each year on Palm Sunday.

To the quiet of that Bethany home Jesus and His disciples returned for rest and refreshment during the week of His passion. The sounds of discord and strife gave way to that healing which is possible among those whose very presence speaks of amiability and mutual trust.

In a second Bethany home an unnamed woman anointed Jesus with precious oint-ment, a gesture which, as Jesus said, would ever after commemorate her loving devotion.

Through Bethany wended the road from Jerusalem to Jericho, forever remembered as the scene of the parable of the good Samaritan and its lesson of a love transcending race and creed and transforming all of God's creation into a neighborhood of loving concern.

Nearby is also that hallowed spot from which Jesus, having blessed His faithful followers, ascended into the heavens. He had promised continuity in the love He had shared with them: "the Father . . . shall give you another Comforter, that he may abide with you for ever" (John 14:16).

THE OPEN DOOR

There passed the low door of His Nazareth
    home
    Men-of-the-earth, women with water jars,
The tinkling camel train, soldiers of Rome;
    And, in the quiet evening, when the stars
Shone over Galilee, shepherds, whose flocks
    Grazed the high hills, moved slowly up
      the street
To take the night-watch where gray, rugged
    rocks
    Gave shade to pasture grasses lush and
      sweet.

And One who watched the anxious world
    go by,
    Dreamed of a door unknown to human
      eye.

He saw its portal—fair, with peace alight;
    Through hungry, troubled throngs the
      pathway led.
Sad faces lifted and dull eyes grew bright
    When, "Follow me . . . I am the door,"
      He said.
Before He felt the scourge and climbed the
    hill
    He knew man's spirit free forevermore;
In spite of death itself He visioned still
    God's kingdom through a lighted, open
      door.

And down the night, ignore it as men will,
    They who bear crosses find it open still.

IDA NORTON MUNSON

❖❖❖

If the tender, profound, and sympathizing
love, practiced and recommended by Jesus,
were paramount in every heart, the loftiest
and most glorious idea of human society
would be realized, and little be wanting to
make this world a kingdom of heaven.

FRIEDRICH ADOLF KRUMMACHER

He saw the hardships, the atrocities, the
injustice, and the disorder.

He saw our false securities and our break-
downs.

He could not stand it any more.

He could not bear any longer being God
on high without being God on earth, our
Helper, Savior, and Redeemer.

And He not only wanted action, He took
it.

This is His kingdom at hand.

He has called us, the unworthy.

He has led us to His house and opened
the door for us.

He even gave us our own key.

He has invited us to His table and given
us of His bread and of His wine.

He has acted like a true Father for us.

KARL BARTH

❖❖❖

THE CENTER

At the center of everything in the Christian religion stands the fact of God's re-
deeming love:

a love that returns not evil for evil but
casts over evil the cloak of its forgiveness;

a love poured, not on the righteous and
self-reliant, but on weak and helpless sinners;

a love given, not as a reward of goodness, but in order to create a goodness which
is its own reward;

a love that goes out to seek us when we
are "yet a great way off";

a love that stoops to conquer and humbles
itself that we may be exalted;

a love that goes with us through the
valley of the shadow of death in order that
we with it may come forth at last into its
own larger life.

JOHN BAILLIE

❖❖❖

AFTER EASTER

"It was here He used to sit
  And here He slept;
And when He heard my brother'd died
  I mind how He wept.

"Here was His low bench,
  And here His bed,"
To the neighbor women
  Martha said.

"He liked the talking,
  And He liked more
To sit silently
  Looking at the floor."

Martha spoke to neighbors
  With pride in her tone.
But Mary in the garden
  Was crying alone.

                    MARY CAROLYN DAVIES

❖❖❖

LOVE FOR THEIR SAKE

How Christ's death takes away thy sins thou
wilt never know on earth—perhaps not in
heaven. It is a mystery which thou must
believe and adore. But why He died thou
canst see at the first glance, if thou hast a
human heart and will look at what God
means thee to look at—Christ upon His
Cross. He died because He was Love—love
itself, love boundless, unconquerable, un-
changeable—love which inhabits eternity,
and therefore could not be hardened or
foiled by any sin or rebellion of man, but
must love men still—must go out to seek and
save them, must dare, suffer any misery,
shame, death itself, for their sake—just because it is absolute and perfect Love which
inhabits eternity.

                    CHARLES KINGSLEY

❖❖❖

Love likes to hear love protest its love. Jesus
appealed to Peter for his personal love, for
his pre-eminent love, and for love principal
and all-important. He was calling Peter to
a ministry of love to meet the world's needs.
The world needs to be shepherded because
all men "like sheep have gone astray." But
they are the sheep for whom the Shepherd
died; He has redeemed them; and they will
learn of His love as His disciples, you and I,
minister to them in love. "Do you love me?
. . . Tend my sheep."

                    TODAY

❖❖❖

Then Jesus came, and the universe flow-
ered. What God had so long looked for at
last He saw—in a human mind that was able
to grasp His purpose, in a human heart that
manifested perfectly the divine quality of
love, in a human will perfectly surrendered
to His will even unto death. And what Jesus
achieved, He achieved not for Himself only,
but, because of that real unity of the human
race in which we are all bound together,
for us all.

                    STEPHEN NEILL

❖❖❖

RENEWAL

These things are beautiful beyond belief—
The pleasant weakness that comes after
  pain;
The radiant greenness that comes after rain;
The deepened faith that follows after grief;
And the awakening to love again.

❖❖❖

At Pentecost they spoke a language which
all nationalities understood. That language
lives. It is called love, and it has never
yet been misunderstood.

                    WILLIAM H. BODDY

❖❖❖

THE FAITH OF JESUS

Jesus bet His life on the love of God, not an easy thing to do—not an easy thing even for Him to do.

He, no less than other men, faced and felt the awful mystery of life, its joy and its sorrow, its beauty and its pain.

It has been said of Him that "misfortune could not reach Him," but it did appear to reach Him in Gethsemane.

It has been claimed that "nothing even for a moment broke the serenity of His life on earth," but something did appear to break it when He cried out, "My God, my God, why hast thou forsaken me?"

The existence of God Jesus took for granted, as did the prophets who came before Him and the whole race of men to which He belonged.

But the love of God He could not take for granted; on that He gambled His life. He staked everything on the belief that love was, is, and ever shall be at the heart of the world.

And He dared to believe that love is power, that it is, indeed, the greatest power in the world, able to overcome the world, destined in the end to rule the world.

This belief in the power of love He was required to hold in the face of many disturbing facts.

There was, for example, Herod, a petty, perfumed tyrant who had cut off the head of the man whom Jesus regarded as the greatest and best He had ever known; and Herod was ruler of the little principality in which Jesus was born and grew to manhood.

There was also Caiaphas, an astute politician wearing the robes of religion but without either the vision of the prophet or the consecration of the priest, caring more for the favor of Caesar than for the approval of God; and Caiaphas occupied the highest ecclesiastical position in Jerusalem.

Far away, but casting a shadow which even the remotest of provinces could feel, was imperial Rome, proud and ruthless, but governing and taxing the world.

His belief in the power of love Jesus was required to hold in the face of formidable facts, but hold it He did until the end.

Now, in my judgment there is no ground for hope that we shall ever have the courage to take the way of Jesus unless we develop the faith of Jesus.

ERNEST FREMONT TITTLE

❖❖❖

HEART'S RESPONSE

Give me a pure heart—that I may see Thee,
A humble heart—that I may hear Thee,
A heart of love—that I may serve Thee,
A heart of faith—that I may abide in Thee.

DAG HAMMARSKJÖLD

❖❖❖

THE MEASURE OF LOVE

Love is the filling from one's own another's
    cup;
Love is the daily laying down and taking
    up;
A choosing of the stony path through each
    new day
That other feet may tread with ease a
    smoother way.
Love is not blind but looks abroad through
    other eyes;
And asks not, "Must I give?" but "May I
    sacrifice?"
Love hides its grief, that other hearts and
    lips may sing;
And burdened walks, that other lives may
    buoyant wing.
Hast thou a love like that within thy soul?
'Twill crown thy life with bliss when thou
    dost reach the goal.

THE P. E. O. RECORD

❖❖❖

LITTLE PRAYER IN APRIL

Thou, kiss-betrayed . . . Thou, friend-
  denied . . .
  Thou—for Thy Love—the crucified,
I waft to Thee this little prayer,
  Upon the fluent April air,
For courage to risk one Judas-kiss—
  Some Peter's denial, lest I miss,
By my cold caution, hurrying on,
  The loving loyalty shown by John.

VIOLET ALLEYN STOREY

❖❖❖

HIS OWN

O God, who made us for Thy own,
We cannot hope for peace apart
From Thee or know true joy until
We bid Thee welcome in our heart.

O God, who made us for mankind,
We have no happiness until
We help to bear our brothers' load,
According to Thy holy will.

GAIL BROOK BURKET

❖❖❖

FROM BETHLEHEM TO CALVARY

From Bethlehem to Calvary the Savior's
  journey lay;
  Doubt, unbelief, scorn, fear, and hate
  beset Him day by day,
But in His heart He bore God's love that
  brightened all the way.

O'er the Judaean hills He walked, serene
  and brave of soul,
  Seeking the beaten paths of men, touching and making whole,
Dying at last for love of man, on Calvary's
  darkened knoll.

He went with patient step and slow, as one
  who scatters seed;
  Like a fierce hunger in His heart He felt
  the world's great need,
And the negations Moses gave He changed
  to loving deed.

From Bethlehem to Calvary the world still
  follows on.
  Even as the halt and blind of old along
  His path were drawn;
Through Calvary's clouds they seek the
  light that led Him to the dawn.

MEREDITH NICHOLSON

❖❖❖

The mercies of God are dispensed out of the
treasury of His goodness, wrought by the
art of His wisdom, effected by the arm of
His power.

STEPHEN CHARNOCK

❖❖❖

To love at all is to be vulnerable.
Love anything and your heart will certainly
  be wrung and possibly be broken.
If you want to make sure of keeping it in-
  tact, you must give your heart to no one,
  not even to an animal.
Wrap it carefully round with hobbies and
  little luxuries; avoid all entanglements;
  lock it up safe in the casket or coffin of
  your selfishness.
But in that casket of your selfishness—safe,
  dark, motionless, airless—it will change.
It will not be broken; it will become un-
  breakable, impenetrable, irredeemable.
The only place outside Heaven where you
  can be perfectly safe from the dangers of
  love is Hell.

C. S. LEWIS

Beer-sheba

. . . there is a place of perfect peace

PEACE

✦✦✦

He maketh me to lie down in green pastures: he leadeth me beside the still waters. He restoreth my soul.

PSALM 23:2–3

And Jacob went out from Beer-sheba, and went toward Haran. And he lighted upon a certain place, and tarried there all night, because the sun was set; and he took of the stones of that place, and put them for his pillows, and lay down in that place to sleep. And he dreamed, and behold a ladder set up on the earth, and the top of it reached to heaven: and behold the angels of God ascending and descending on it. And, behold, the Lord stood above it, and said, I am the Lord God of Abraham thy father, and the God of Isaac. . . . And, behold, I am with thee, and will keep thee in all places whither thou goest. . . . And Jacob awaked out of his sleep, and he said, Surely the Lord is in this place; and I knew it not.

GENESIS 28:10–13, 15–16

Thou wilt keep him in perfect peace, whose mind is stayed on thee: because he trusteth in thee.

ISAIAH 26:3

Peace I leave with you, my peace I give unto you: not as the world giveth, give I unto you. Let not your heart be troubled, neither let it be afraid.

JOHN 14:27

✦✦✦

MEDITATION

Seven deep wells account for the ancient attractiveness of Beer-sheba to the patriarchs and their descendants. At this place Abraham made a covenant of peace with his erstwhile foe Abimelech, which was renewed a generation later by their sons. On his flight to Haran, Jacob made his peace with God nearby, and many years later he returned to Beer-sheba to offer a sacrifice before journeying to Egypt to be reunited with his son Joseph.

Peace is a many-splendored biblical word which speaks of a divine and human relatedness and harmony that are both inner and outer, horizontal and vertical. "Seek peace and pursue it," urged the prophet Isaiah, and the psalmist wrote, "In quietness and confidence shall be your strength."

Christian peace is more than a mere absence of disturbance and discord; it is living in a manner consistent with the will and purpose of God. This precious gift of God through Him who is the Prince of Peace endows the believer with an inner feeling of tranquillity and contentment such as the world can neither give nor take away.

As one who searches deserts, dune on dune,
And finds but skulls and vulture wings, ac-
    cursed
With loneliness and heat of blazing noon—
So seeks the mind of man. How deep his
    thirst!
What alien countries, far and strange, his
    heart,
A prodigal, explores—to taste their wine,
And feasts one brief wild hour, till stripped,
    apart,
His hunger fain would share the husks with
    swine.
For these are restless things, the heart, the
    mind,
Whose old, old longings drive them east
    and west
Across the centuries until they find
The Living Water, Bread of Life—and rest.
For here alone is home, and man is stilled—
His thirsting quenched, his heart's long
    hunger filled.

LESLIE SAVAGE CLARK

❖❖❖

ALONE INTO THE MOUNTAIN

All day from that deep well of life within
    Himself has He drawn healing for the
    press
Of folk, restoring strength, forgiving sin,
    Quieting frenzy, comforting distress.
Shadows of evening fall, yet wildly still
    They throng Him, touch Him, clutch His
    garment's hem,
Fall down and clasp His feet, cry on Him,
    till
    The Master, spent, slips from the midst
    of them
And climbs the mountain for a cup of peace,
    Taking a sheer and rugged track untrod
Save by a poor lost sheep with thorn-torn
    fleece
    That follows on and hears Him talk with
    God.

KATHARINE LEE BATES

From SONGS OF JESUS

O sing a song of Galilee,
    Of lake and woods and hill,
Of Him who walked upon the sea
    And bade its waves be still:
For though, like waves on Galilee,
    Dark seas of trouble roll,
When faith has heard the Master's word
    Falls peace upon the soul.

LOUIS F. BENSON

❖❖❖

FAITH AND SERENITY

Abraham began his journey without any
knowledge of his ultimate destination. He
obeyed a noble impulse without any dis-
cernment of its consequences. He took
"one step," and he did not "ask to see the
distant scene."

And that is faith, to do God's will here
and now, quietly leaving the results to Him.

Faith is not concerned with the entire
chain; its devoted attention is fixed upon
the immediate link.

Faith is not knowledge of a moral process;
it is fidelity in a moral act.

Faith leaves something to the Lord; it
obeys His immediate commandment and
leaves to Him direction and destiny.

And so faith is accompanied by serenity.
"He that believeth shall not make haste"—
or, more literally, "shall not get into a fuss."
He shall not get into a panic, neither fetch-
ing fears from his yesterdays nor from his
tomorrows.

Concerning his yesterdays faith says,
"Thou hast beset me behind."

Concerning his tomorrows faith says,
"Thou has beset me before."

Concerning his today faith says, "Thou
hast laid thine hand upon me." That is
enough, just to feel the pressure of the
guiding hand.

JOHN HENRY JOWETT

❖❖❖

The ultimate key to human history is not in the hands of men with their nuclear weapons but in the pierced hands of the Prince of Peace.

FRANK E. GAEBELEIN

❖❖❖

MAY PETER'S CHOICE BE OURS

If Thou art not the answer, there is no
    answer.
Lord, to whom shall we go?
If there were a wide range of acceptable
    choices
Through which we might pick our way care-
    fully
And decide after prolonged reflection
And with due regard to all the factors in-
    volved—
If we were given a chance to turn the matter
    over in our minds,
If we could test this or that theory
Under differing circumstances over a pe-
    riod of time—
If we had an opportunity to study the lan-
    guages
And philosophies of all the world,
Before deciding whether or not it is true
That Thou hast the words of eternal life,
We might come to some well-thought-out
    conclusion.
Unfortunately it is not like this.
If Thou art not the answer, there is no
    answer.
The middle ground has collapsed; there is
    only heaven or the abyss.

EDITH LOVEJOY PIERCE

❖❖❖

OUR BOATS ARE SMALL

O Maker of the mighty deep,
    Whereon our vessels fare,
Above our life's adventure keep
    Thy faithful watch and care.
In Thee we trust, whate'er befall;
Thy sea is great, our boats are small.

We know not where the secret tides
    Will help us or delay,
Nor where the lurking tempest hides,
    Nor where the fogs are gray.
We trust in Thee, whate'er befall;
Thy sea is great, our boats are small.

When outward bound we boldly sail
    And leave the friendly shore,
Let not our hearts of courage fail
    Until the voyage is o'er.
We trust in Thee, whate'er befall;
Thy sea is great, our boats are small.

When homeward bound, we gladly turn,
    Oh! bring us safely there,
Where harbor lights of friendship burn
    And peace is in the air.
We trust in Thee, whate'er befall;
Thy sea is great, our boats are small.

Beyond the circle of the sea,
    When voyaging is past,
We seek our final port in Thee;
    Oh! bring us home at last.
In Thee we trust, whate'er befall;
Thy sea is great, our boats are small.

HENRY VAN DYKE

❖❖❖

ONLY ONE KING

In arrogance and vanity
Kings sculpture regal words and creeds
On granite that posterity
May marvel at their mighty deeds
Of war and conquest; time and rust
Grind these memorials to dust.

Only one King came scorning power,
Walked with the humble of the land
And served mankind His willing hour:
And He wrote only on the sand!

JOHN RICHARD MORELAND

✛✛✛

PEACE

There is a peace that cometh after sorrow,
  Of hope surrendered, not of hope ful-
    filled;
A peace that looketh not upon tomorrow,
  But calmly on a tempest that is stilled.
A peace which lives not now in joy's ex-
    cesses,
  Nor in the happy life of love secure;
But in the unerring strength the heart pos-
    sesses
  Of conflicts won while learning to en-
    dure.
A peace there is in sacrifice secluded;
  A life subdued, from will and passion
    free.
'Tis not the peace which over Eden
    brooded,
  But that which triumphed in Gethsem-
    ane.

JESSIE ROSE GATES

✛✛✛

THE SOUL'S GARDEN

Every soul that is truly alive has a garden of which no other holds the key; and in hours of weariness, when it is breathless with the hot race of life, and harassed by a babel of voices, it slips through the gate and walks at peace among the flowers.

There is a garden of the soul also, of which that beyond the brook Kedron is the type, where Jesus walks with His disciples, and the clash of the world cannot drown the music of His voice.

It was said of the garden on the farther side of Kedron that "Jesus ofttimes resorted thither with His disciples"; and when the High Priest's servants sought to convict Peter of his discipleship, they clinched their appeal with, "Did not I see thee in the garden with Him?"

And still the true Christian disciple is a man of the garden. He carries with him a breath of the pure, invigorating, fragrant air that blows across the secret garden of communion.

The sound of its crystal fountains is in his voice; the radiance of its sunlit flowers is mirrored in his eyes. He is not as other men are; he carries a garden in his heart, and his fellows take knowledge of him that he has been with Jesus.

In the garden of communion the clamor of the world and the contendings of the Church are alike unheard.

No sound of controversy penetrates that enclosed sanctuary; no rivalries can live within its gates of peace.

There the Twelve clamor no longer for the highest place in the Kingdom; there Peter steps out of the shallows of impetuosity into the clear depths of love, John unlearns on the bosom of his Lord the passion that would call down fire from heaven, and Philip's questionings are lost in a certainty deeper than that of the inquiring mind.

Small wonder that the disciples loved the garden, and that disciples of all ages have been loth to exchange its sweet intimacies for the rough and irritating traffic of the open road! It belonged at once to the strength and to the weakness of medieval sainthood that it lingered so persistently in the garden.

EMILY HERMAN
From THE SECRET GARDEN OF THE SOUL
AND OTHER DEVOTIONAL WRITINGS

✛✛✛

THE PLACE OF PEACE

At the heart of the cyclone tearing the sky
And flinging the clouds and the towers by,
  Is a place of central calm:
So here in the roar of mortal things,
I have a place where my spirit sings,
  In the hollow of God's Palm.

EDWIN MARKHAM

✛✛✛

Lord! in this peaceful place
    I lift my heart to Thee;
How calm the hour, how safe the path,
    If Thou wilt walk with me.

Beside the Syrian sea,
    And in the desert rude,
'Mid silence was Thy spirit nursed,
    And steeled with solitude.

'Twas joy and strength to Thee
    Man's fellowship to share—
The welcome of a village friend,
    Or Martha's loving care.

Lord, I would learn of Thee
    As here with friends I meet,
And in the silence of the hills
    Would find refreshment sweet.

Amid these tranquil vales,
    Or by the wave-lapped shore,
Make Thou this hallowed place to me
    Emmaus as of yore.

                    FREDERICK J. GILLMAN

❖❖❖

THE FRIENDLY UNIVERSE

God of the rainbow, the seedtime and
    harvest,
    Summer and winter, the cold and the
    heat,
Swinging the earth through the arc of the
    seasons,
    Like a great pendulum hung at Thy
    feet;

Drilling the ranks of the stars' shining
    legions
    Till they keep time on the highways of
    space,
Making the mote and the mightiest moun-
    tain
    Bend to the glory that holds them in
    place;

Thine is the kingdom, the power and
    glory,
    Ours to walk steadily, world without
    end,
Free from blind chance or the whims of a
    tyrant
    In the dependable house of a friend!

                    EDWIN O. KENNEDY

❖❖❖

There can be no peace on earth until we
have learned to respect the dignity of man
and are willing to build on the foundation
of human love the kind of world that the
great teachers of mankind have portrayed
to us from the time of the Ten Commandments and the Sermon on the Mount.
These are the true lessons of mortal life.

                    DAVID LAWRENCE

❖❖❖

THE LIGHT WITHIN

Within the window of my heart,
    For all the world to see,
There is a candle lit against
    The night's immensity.

It cannot change the night to day,
    Nor conquer fog and rain;
It holds the armies of the dark
    Outside the window-pane.

Who sees its light, or where it shines,
    Only God can know;
The boundless legions of the gloom
    Cannot quench its glow.

                    EARL BIGELOW BROWN

❖❖❖

WISDOM AND LOVE

God illumines the world with His wisdom
and excites it to the love of Himself.

                    PIERRE ABÉLARD

Bethsaida

. . . . I have called you friends

FRIENDS

❖❖❖

SCRIPTURE

The day following Jesus would go forth into Galilee, and findeth Philip, and saith unto him, Follow me. Now Philip was of Beth-saida, the city of Andrew and Peter. Philip findeth Nathanael, and saith unto him, We have found him, of whom Moses in the law, and the prophets, did write, Jesus of Nazareth, the son of Joseph. . . . Come and see.

JOHN 1:43–46

The soul of Jonathan was knit with the soul of David, and Jonathan loved him as his own soul. . . . Then Jonathan and David made a covenant, because he loved him as his own soul. And Jonathan stripped himself of the robe that was upon him, and gave it to David, and his garments, even to his sword, and to his bow, and to his girdle.

I SAMUEL 18:1, 3–4

This is my commandment, That ye love one another, as I have loved you. Greater love hath no man than this, that a man lay down his life for his friends. Ye are my friends, if ye do whatsoever I command you. Henceforth I call you not servants; for the servant knoweth not what his lord doeth: but I have called you friends; for all things that I have heard of my Father I have made known unto you.

JOHN 15:12–15

❖❖❖

MEDITATION

Few words reflect greater warmth and inspiration than those of our Lord: "Ye are my friends." A friend of publicans and sinners, Jesus solicits our friendship and offers His own, saying, "Him that cometh to me I will in no wise cast out."

Multitudes have sung the encouraging words of such favorite hymns as "What a Friend we have in Jesus." To know Christ as a friend, which according to John 15:14 means that we do what he tells us to do, hallows all relationships and brings into a bond of loving friendship the world-wide community of Christians.

Bethsaida is emblematic of Christian friendship, for this fishing town near the northern end of the Sea of Galilee was the home of the disciple Philip and of Jesus' beloved companions, the brothers Peter and Andrew, fishing associates of James and John. Jesus undoubtedly made frequent visits to the home of Peter, and rambunctious Peter illustrates how the alchemy of friendship transforms a hot-tempered and impulsive individual into a man of dedication, loyalty, and self-sacrificing devotion.

43

BY AN ANCIENT SEA

Here, on this sunny shore, in simpler days
  A Wise Man walked, communing with
    His friends.
He loved these quiet waters, and the
    flowers
  That flecked those fields with blue and
    gold. What hours
Of thoughtful talk were theirs—of Him
    who sends
  Earth's summer beauty; of the varied
    ways
Of human life; and of the life to be.
  They understood his words—those sim-
    ple men;
No futile argument or sophistry
  Ensnared and vexed their minds. Oh,
    that again
This Man might talk to us, and know our
    needs!
  Alas, His voice is drowned by jangling
    creeds!

THOMAS CURTIS CLARK

❖❖❖

THE GREAT COMPANIONSHIP

If we open the Bible, we find men living in intimate companionship with God—men like ourselves, a little weak, a little strong, a little good, a little bad, foolish when we fancy we are wise and wise when we fear we are foolish, wayward, willful, stupid—but each of us held to God by a personal tie.

That was what religion meant to them. They had friendly dealings with God.

In discouragement, He was a friend that helped; if defeated, He saved them from despair.

They talked to Him and He heard; they trusted Him and were not betrayed. They and God were friends.

When He was near, the trees clapped their hands; if He seemed far away they were forlorn.

One misses that sense of intimacy with God today.

It seems more difficult to be friendly with God, but that is only seeming—He is as near, as real, as available, and as ineffable today as ever He was in the days agone.

JOSEPH FORT NEWTON

❖❖❖

AFTER THE CRUCIFIXION

We were the children Jesus loved.
Jonathan sat upon His knee
That morning in the marketplace
Of Galilee.

Benjamin was the little boy
Who had the lunch of fish and bread
Which Jesus blessed—and Benjamin saw
Five thousand fed.

And Miriam was sick, and slept
And would not wake—and she can tell
How Jesus came and took her hand,
And she was well!

We were all children, everywhere,
Who looked upon His face. We knew,
That day they told us He had died,
It was not true.

We wondered why our parents wept
And doubted Him and were deceived,
For we remembered what He said,
And we believed!

SARA HENDERSON HAY

❖❖❖

WORLD'S JOY

The joy of this world, when you have summed it up, is found in the making of friends.

WILLIAM C. WOLFMULLER

From THE FRIEND'S BURIAL

The dear Lord's best interpreters
   Are humble human souls;
The gospel of a life like His
   Is more than books or scrolls.

From scheme and creed the light goes out,
   The saintly fact survives;
The blessed Master none can doubt,
   Revealed in holy lives.

             JOHN GREENLEAF WHITTIER

SHARING

The roses red upon my neighbor's vine
Are owned by him, but they are also mine.
His was the cost and his the labor, too;
But mine and his their loveliness to view.
They bloom for me, and are for me as fair
As for the man who gives them all his care.
Thus I am rich, because a good man grew
A rose-clad vine for all his neighbors' view.
I know from this that others plant for me,
And what they own my joy may also be.
So why be selfish when so much that's fine
Is grown for you upon your neighbor's
   vine.

                    A. L. GRUGER

As our Master and Leader, Jesus seeks our company, not in order to discourage us by His superiority, but to raise us above ourselves through our participation in His spirit. Jesus lives for men. For this reason do men live for Jesus. Freely and royally we may take from Him what we can receive from Him yet today, as we can obtain them from no other source: renewal of life for ourselves, fulfillment of our ideals for our world, and ultimate union with God.

             FRIEDRICH RITTELMEYER

THE ROAD TO EMMAUS

Twilight. And on a dusty ribboned way,
   Out from Jersualem, two travelers
     walked.
Gray shadows touched their feet, but
     deeper lay
   The shadows in their hearts. They softly
     talked
Of days just passed, of hopeless days in
     view,
   Of boats, of nets, the while their eyes
     were dim,
Of Galilee, the work they used to do;
   Their voices often stilled, remembering
     Him.

A Stranger also walked that way, and when
   They sensed His nearness, some new
     sympathy
Assuaged their grief. Old hopes came
     warm again
   As, in the dusk, He kept them com-
     pany . . .
Thus, through the troubled twilight of
     today
   Emmaus road has stretched its shining
     thread,
And still Christ walks beside men on the
     way,
   To hold the light of hope, to break the
     bread.

             IDA NORTON MUNSON

AS PETER LOVED

As Peter loved I love, and in his fashion:
   With boastful promises and bursts of
     passion;
Then anxious waverings and hot denials,
   And faith that drowns amid a sea of
     trials.
Yet strong beyond my fitful love I see
   His love forever reaching out to me.

             JEAN HOGAN DUDLEY

❖❖❖

MEDITATION ON JESUS CHRIST

He enters my mind and laughs. We talk
  thought-talk
  About the fish and Peter's boat, the nets
Always in need of mending; Thomas' balk
  In faith; and Judas' fall; the triumphs,
    regrets;
Good wine from water; many sleepless
  nights—
  But, not all spent in sorrow: friends
    out-stay
The moon when voices roll, and wisdom
  bites
  At wisdom, making every mind a prey.
He speaks about the Twelve, their varied
  views,
  Their loyalty, the curse of coin. He
    sighs,
Then smiles, recalls how Mary would refuse
  To help good Martha, Martha's angry
    eyes.
He brings the strength of laughter and
  quells my fears—
  Despite the Cross, not all of life is tears.

JOHANNA RACHEL BRANIGAN

❖❖❖

THE TOUCH OF JESUS

One touch of Jesus makes all the world
kin. That is true in the common practical
give-and-take. One touch of Jesus reveals
the fact that all the race is kin. He in-
directly makes clear the essential unity of
the race.

There is a peculiar separateness between
the East and the West. It persists, tenaciously, intangibly, unchangeably, despite
contacts of commerce and travel.

Men are always more alike than different. But the differences do stare one in
the face, and are apt to rub him the wrong
way.

That separateness makes the humanness
of Jesus—innate, instinctive, distinctive
humanness—stand out sharply. A West-
erner, by blood and breeding, in intimate
continued touch, feels it keenly as he
sojourns in the East.

The exclusive Chinese, the conservative
Briton, the dark-eyed, quick-tongued Latin
of the south of Europe, the flaxen-haired,
rugged-speeched Scandinavian; the intense
Gallic, either north or south of the Pyre-
nees; the phlegmatic Hollander, all alike
glow, and glow together, in heart and eye
and tongue when in touch with Jesus.

The Alpine mountaineer, the dike-
dwelling lowlander, Swiss and Hollander,
join together in heart unity, with city
dweller, and the tiller of the soil, and with
the savage-born kraal dweller, and their
hearts burn with a common fire, when
touched by the human touch of Jesus.

S. D. GORDON

❖❖❖

All the glory and beauty of Christ are
manifested within, and there He delights
to dwell. His visits there are frequent, His
condescension amazing, His conversation
sweet, His comforts refreshing, and the
peace that He brings passeth all understanding.

THOMAS A KEMPIS

❖❖❖

MAINSPRING

I can hardly conceive of life
without friends.
It would seem to be life
without light.
At the highest peaks of our civilization,
friendship has always been in great esteem
and has been one of the mainsprings
of creative activity.
I think I would define friendship
as the mutual good will
between two persons,
each for the other's sake.

BRUNO SCOTT JAMES

THE GOSPEL OF "WE"

The "we" spirit is the very essence of Christianity. It takes at least two people to practice the teachings of Christ. Jesus said that love to God and love to one's neighbor was the summing up of all the law and the prophets. He announced that "where two or three are gathered together in my name there am I in the midst." Notice that the lowest number is two, that it takes at least yourself and somebody else and God to form this trinity. When Jesus sent His disciples out He sent them two by two. Thus we have again exemplified the "we" spirit.

EDGAR DE WITT JONES

❖❖❖

Christ ever took men on their strongest side.

He accepted the highest in them as representing their true self.

He believed the best of them, and so despaired of none but hoped for all.

He discovered soul, however buried in sense.

In the company of sinners He dreamed of saints.

HUGH BLACK

❖❖❖

A FAITHFUL FRIEND

A faithful friend is a strong defence; and he that hath found such an one hath found a treasure.

There is nothing that can be taken in exchange for a faithful friend; and his excellency is beyond price.

A faithful friend is a medicine of life; and they that fear the Lord shall find him.

He that feareth the Lord directeth his friendship aright; for as he is, so is his neighbour also.

ECCLESIASTICUS 6:14–17

INTIMATE STRANGER

The Stranger had a way with Him,
    The time He tarried in our place;
The children ran to play with Him,
    And something in His storied face
Made old folk wish to stay with Him
    Whose memory with their tales kept pace.

Not one but did confide in Him
    The inmost thought He ever had;
The wayward owned a guide in Him,
    To lead them out of mazes mad;
It seemed there was a side in Him
    For wise or wild, for sad or glad.

He lived apart—was near to us,
    Was intimate and stranger, too!
He ever grew more dear to us;
    Yet, only when He bade adieu,
The secret was made clear to us!
    And we, at last, The Poet knew!

EDITH M. THOMAS

❖❖❖

WE HAVE BROKEN OUR BREAD TOGETHER

We have broken our bread together and now we part,
    We have broken the bread of the mind and the bread of the heart,
We may never meet again till another star,
    But we shall be friends together wherever we are.

There is no time for lamenting, no moment for sighs,
    Let us trust and be glad, see the truth in each other's eyes,
Let us smile as we wave farewell where the long road bends,
    Let us sing to the vow that makes us forever friends.

EDWIN MARKHAM

48

Capernaum

. . . according to your faith

FAITH

✥✥✥

SCRIPTURE

The word is nigh thee, even in thy mouth, and in thy heart: that is, the word of faith.

ROMANS 10:8

And when Jesus was entered into Capernaum, there came unto him a centurion, beseeching him, and saying, Lord, my servant lieth at home sick of the palsy, grievously tormented. And Jesus saith unto him, I will come and heal him. The centurion answered and said, Lord, I am not worthy that thou shouldest come under my roof: but speak the word only, and my servant shall be healed. . . . When Jesus heard it, he marvelled, and said to them that followed, Verily I say unto you, I have not found so great faith, no, not in Israel. . . . And Jesus said unto the centurion, Go thy way; and as thou hast believed, so be it done unto thee. And his servant was healed in the selfsame hour.

MATTHEW 8:5–8, 10, 13

Be thou faithful unto death, and I will give thee a crown of life.

REVELATION 2:10

✥✥✥

MEDITATION

Christian faith is trust in and reliance upon Christ. Those who believed in Him were gathered by Him into a fellowship of faith.

After the people of His hometown, Nazareth, rejected Him, Jesus made Capernaum the focal center of His Galilean ministry, and in time Capernaum became known as "his own city."

In this community of some size and importance He called Matthew from a tax collector's seat to be a disciple. Nearby He called fishermen to become "fishers of men."

Here, speaking to great multitudes, He became a popular leader and taught in the local synagogue and elsewhere, where He spoke some of His most memorable words, including the discourse on the Bread of Life which followed the feeding of the five thousand.

Capernaum was the scene of many of Christ's faith healings, including that of a centurion's servant, a demoniac, a paralytic, Peter's mother-in-law, and a nobleman's son.

The inspiration of those whose faith was confirmed by the Master's touch and word has stirred generations of people to faith in Christ.

Ironically, His mighty works did not bring to repentance the people of Capernaum, and today only weathered ruins mark the place.

Galilee speaks in the wind today,
    And fisherman's talk is on its breath,
The Lord is walking on Presqu'ile Bay—
    The Lord who conquered death.
The nets of Peter are on this shore,
    Singing low by a fresh sea-wall
The voice of Stephen is at my door,
    And yon's the boat of the shipwrecked
        Paul.

Thomas the Doubter, still in doubt,
    Walks the shale in a fearful way,
Nor heeds the call of his Lord, "Come out,
    And walk with me upon Presqu'ile
        Bay."
The shore is dark with an ancient horde:
    Here's Bartimaeus, now keen of eye;
And here comes Mary to greet her Lord,
    Running the waves with a joyous cry.

Across this Bay of the Singing Sands
    Nearer and nearer the Master comes,
And Pilate goes down to wash his hands,
    And outcasts wait for the fallen crumbs.
But the priests and the rabbis, as of old,
    Pore over their laws and creeds, and say,
With learned lips that are hard and cold,
    "The Lord walks not on Presqu'ile
        Bay."

If you would behold a Cross arise,
    As once, on an ancient day, it rose,
Say to the rich and the proud and the wise,
    "The Lord over Presqu'ile Bay now
        goes."
And, as of old, upon every hand
    The fools will laugh, for they cannot see
That all the earth is a Holy Land,
    And every water is Galilee.

                    WILSON MAC DONALD

❖❖❖

SON OF MAN

He was born in a manger, lived as a peasant, slept out on the ground at times
when nothing better offered. "The foxes
had holes, the birds of the air had nests,
but the Son of Man had nowhere to lay
His head."

He worked with His hands in a carpenter shop until He was thirty years old.

He never was in Greece in His life; He
probably never read a line of Homer or
Plato. Yet He learned to speak as man
never spake, and His words have been
translated into all tongues men speak.

He was not even a Roman citizen, but
rather a subject of the Roman Empire in
an obscure province. Yet He made that
small country where He lived the Holy
Land for all time.

He never saw a real city, for Jerusalem,
then as now, was only a country town. Yet
His Cross is bravely outlined against the
sky in every city on earth.

What a life it was! He accepted Himself
and went out to do the will of One who
sent Him, and look at the result!

He became the Perfect, the Typal, the
Representative Man, the Son of Man, because He lived out His own true, best,
complete self.

                    CHARLES R. BROWN

❖❖❖

MASTER OF THE MULTITUDE

O Master of the multitude,
    Toilworn, dust-stained and tanned,
The rich and poor, refined and rude,
    Of every time and land—
Come, walk with us and talk with us,
    And share our grief and woe;
O Master of the multitude,
    Teach us Thy love to know.

O Master of the multitude,
    The millions wander still
Without a guide, without a light,
    Without an aim or will—
Come, walk with us and talk with us
    Among our people move;
O Master of the multitude,
    Redeem us by Thy love.

                    CHAUNCEY R. PIETY

❖❖❖

The more we realize that Christ must be all to us and in us, the more we shall learn to live the real life of faith.

ANDREW MURRAY

❖❖❖

DOUBLE SEARCH

Our search for God is not a one-way traffic. On Jacob's ladder there was a coming down as well as a going up.

While we are seeking God, God is no less seeking us, and it is because God is seeking us that we are seeking Him. Our search is our answer to His approach.

In all living religious action, there is always a convergence of two movements, the Godward movement of man, the manward movement of God.

The one is inconceivable without the other. As well explain man's search for God and leave out God's search for man as explain the movement of the tides and leave out the attraction of the moon.

God comes to man; man comes to God; and there is a meeting; and that meeting is on God's side a moment of revelation, and on man's side a moment of discovery.

RICHARD ROBERTS

❖❖❖

MY MASTER'S FACE

No pictured likeness of my Lord have I;
He carved no record of His ministry
    On wood or stone.
He left no sculptured tomb nor parchment dim,
But trusted for all memory of Him
    Men's hearts alone.

Who sees the face but sees in part; who reads
The spirit which it hides, sees all; he needs
    No more. Thy grace—

Thy life in my life, Lord, give Thou to me;
And then, in truth, I may forever see
    My Master's face!

WILLIAM HURD HILLYER

❖❖❖

No one can be truly united with Christ, practicing His lessons, submitting to His yoke of restraint, without realizing that which he can never express in words.

ELLEN G. WHITE

❖❖❖

ONLY BELIEVE

Jesus said that men had only to believe the wonderful news for it to be true; they had only to believe that they were sons of God to be sons of God; they had only to believe that God was their Father to find Him their Father.

That was all: only to believe. But for Jesus to believe was to know.

With this wonderful news Jesus went to Capernaum, on the shore of the lake of Galilee.

Round about that city He proclaimed His message: and crowds flocked to Him.

Sometimes He spoke to them inland, sometimes by the side of the lake.

The substance of what He said was this: "The Kingdom of God is coming now. To enter you must become a son of God. To become a son of God, you must believe you are a son of God. To believe you are a son of God means this: that you must trust your Father utterly, and behave to every man as to a beloved brother, knowing that he also is a son of God."

J. MIDDLETON MURRY

❖❖❖

Faith is the eye that sees Him,
the hand that clings to Him,
the receiving power that appropriates Him.

J. E. WOODBRIDGE

PICTURE OF GOD

The word God is only a picture-frame. All its value depends on the quality of portrait which the frame encloses.

Into that old frame Jesus put a new picture so beautiful because of His own life, so inspiring and winsome because of His sacrificial death, that men never had so thought of God before and never since have been so moved, melted, and transformed by any other thought of Him. That is an amazing thing to have done.

In this world where so many have groped after God, guessed about God, philosophized concerning God, the Master has lived a life of such self-authenticating spiritual grandeur that increasing millions of men when they wish to think about God can think nothing so true, so satisfactory, so adequate, as that the God they worship is like Christ.

Even Paul, who had been brought up in the Old Testament's noblest ideas of God, gained a new name for Him when he had met the Master: "The God and Father of the Lord Jesus."

HARRY EMERSON FOSDICK

❖❖❖

The glory of Jesus is not that He was a certain character in history nineteen hundred years ago but that He can enter into our hearts today and demonstrate His power in our experience.

What the early disciples found in Him, we find.

His radiant humanity sheds its light upon us.

His sinlessness is our perfect ideal.

He is God's prophet, our authoritative teacher.

He is our high priest, our sin offering. He bore our sins upon the tree.

In our hearts we crown Him king. He is our Lord and our God.

WALTER POPE BINNS

TESTIMONY

I cannot fail to be thrilled every time I read the things that Jesus said, and I am more and more convinced of the necessity of following Him. What Jesus means to me is this: in Him we are able to see God and to understand His feelings toward us.

CHARLES SCHULZ

❖❖❖

HIS GARMENT'S HEM

O Blessed Lord, I stoop to Thy flowing
    garment,
    I reach a timid hand to touch its hem
Here among the throng that is surging,
    pressing
    Close about Thee, and I the humblest
    of them.
Then lo, He speaks, and His voice is kind
    and gentle:
    "Who in this throng has touched me?"
    questions He;

And I, who have been needing it so, move
    forward
    To receive the wondrous gift He is
    giving me:
The gift of healing for body, mind and
    spirit,
    The gift of virtue from His own life
    to mine,
And He speaks the blessed words of com-
    mendation:
    "Thy faith hath made thee whole." O
    words that shine
Like silver light to pierce the clouding
    darkness,
    Humbly, indeed, I bow before that
    praise.

Grant me, O blessed One, the strength to
    follow
Thee closer—with greater faith through-
    out my days.

GRACE NOLL CROWELL

54

❖❖❖

Faith is the daring of the soul to go farther than it can see.

WILLIAM NEWTON CLARK

❖❖❖

PRAYER

O Rock of Ages, we who are storm-tossed and buffeted by the tempest of circumstances, come to Thee for refuge.

O Sun Forever Shining, we who walk amid the shadows and the chill of time, come to Thee for light and warmth.

O Great Physician, we who are sick with disappointment and wounded by adversity, come to Thee for the healing of our wounds and the cure of our ills.

O Infinite Wisdom, we who are so beset by ignorance about matters great and small, come to Thee to learn the way of righteousness and truth.

O Loving Heart, we who need compassion and understanding more than anything else, seek that fellowship with Thee who alone can answer the hunger of our hearts.

O Infinite Patience, we who have so often sinned against Thee, come once more asking for forgiveness.

O Limitless Strength, we who are so weak and inadequate, so often broken by our heavy burdens and snared by our temptations, come to Thee for victory.

ALBERT EDWARD DAY

❖❖❖

DIVINE ENERGY

Faith is the energy
your Master gives you,
which enables you
to take hold of His promises
and participate in His life.

PHILIPPE VERNIER

❖❖❖

THE STRANGER

A Stranger came to Bethlehem,
    With great gifts in His hands.
But many people only saw
    A babe in swaddling bands.

A Stranger lived in Nazareth,
    And in His heart was Truth.
But many thought Him Joseph's son,
    An ordinary youth.

A Stranger taught in Galilee,
    With wisdom from on high.
To many He was just a man,
    And so they passed Him by.

That Stranger walks the world today,
    In hearts that have received
The Son of God. No Stranger, He,
    To those who have believed!

HELEN FRAZEE-BOWER

❖❖❖

THE STREAM OF FAITH

From heart to heart, from creed to creed,
    The hidden river runs;
It quickens all the ages down,
    It binds the sires to sons,—
The stream of faith, whose source is God,
    Whose sound, the sound of prayer,
Whose meadows are the holy lives
    Upspringing everywhere.

And still it moves, a broadening flood;
    And fresher, fuller grows
A sense as if the sea were near,
    Toward which the river flows!
O Thou, who art the secret Source
    That rises in each soul,
Thou art the Ocean, too—Thy charm
    That ever-deepening roll!

WILLIAM C. GANNETT

Gethsemane

. . . rendezvous with God

DEVOTION

❖❖❖

SCRIPTURE

Your Father knoweth what things ye have need of, before ye ask him. After this manner therefore pray ye: Our Father which art in heaven, Hallowed be thy name. Thy kingdom come. Thy will be done in earth, as it is in heaven. Give us this day our daily bread. And forgive us our debts, as we forgive our debtors. And lead us not into temptation, but deliver us from evil: For thine is the kingdom, and the power, and the glory, for ever. Amen.

MATTHEW 6:8–13

I will therefore that men pray every where, lifting up holy hands, without wrath and doubting.

I TIMOTHY 2:8

Then cometh Jesus with them unto a place called Gethsemane, and saith unto the disciples, Sit ye here, while I go and pray yonder. . . . And he went a little farther, and fell on his face, and prayed, saying, O my Father, if it be possible, let this cup pass from me: nevertheless not as I will, but as thou wilt. . . . He went away again the second time, and prayed, saying, O my Father, if this cup may not pass away from me, except I drink it, thy will be done.

MATTHEW 26:36, 39, 42

❖❖❖

MEDITATION

The Holy Land might be described on the basis of those places where Jesus prayed, for the Gospels not only identify His praying at each watershed experience in His life but also tell us how He resorted to the refreshment, re-creation, and re-invigoration which prayer provides as a daily and habitual practice. His life was characterized by perpetual communion with His Father.

Jesus taught that "men ought always to pray," and by lesson and example He showed that our prayer life requires sincerity, persistence, humility, submission, and a deep flowing faith that God both hears and responds.

So pervasive is prayer as a spiritual privilege and discipline that Luther wrote, "Prayer is the daily business of a Christian."

It was not as a stranger to the holy habit of prayer that Jesus went into the Garden of Gethsemane in His hour of greatest crisis and decision. Jesus had frequently gone with His disciples to that relatively small place at or near the foot of the Mount of Olives and close to the Kidron.

In Gethsemane Jesus showed His followers how through prayer God gives to those who trust Him the strength and courage both to accept and to accomplish whatever divine purpose He may have for their lives.

GETHSEMANE

All those who journey, soon or late,
    Must pass within the garden's gate;
Must kneel alone in darkness there,
    And battle with some fierce despair.
God pity those who cannot say:
    "Not mine but thine"; who only pray:
"Let this cup pass," and cannot see
    The purpose in Gethsemane.

ELLA WHEELER WILCOX

SECRET SPRINGS

At no time in the experience of the Master was prayer more urgently a part of His being than at the time of His passion. In the Garden of Gethsemane, and later upon the cross, prayer was the warp woven in with the woof of sacrifice that made the redemptive act possible. Without the sustaining courage of prayer He could not have walked the road that led down into a valley where the fires burned white hot, where His naked soul was seared with agony. Only His faith sustained Him when every star in the heavens was blotted out, and that faith found its secret springs back in the hills where He had learned to pray.

WILLIAM E. PHIFER, JR.

From THE CONTINUING CHRIST

Beyond the sea is Galilee
    And ways which Jesus trod,
And hidden there are those high hills
    Where He communed with God;
Yet on the plains of common life,
    Through all the world of men,
The voice that once said, "Follow me,"
    Speaks to our hearts again.

WALTER RUSSELL BOWIE

OPEN THOU MINE EYES

Help me not to miss the splendor
    In the commonplace, I pray.
Lord, I ask for inner vision
    As I walk in faith today.
There are blessings all around me
    Reaching out for me to see;
Give me sight to recognize them,
    All the good Thou hast for me.

Let my gratitude be constant,
    Let my heart respond with praise;
Let a prayer of thanks be given
    For the manifested ways
Thou dost show Thy daily guidance,
    Thy protection, and Thy care.
"Open Thou mine eyes," dear Father,
    To Thy presence everywhere.

DELLA ADAMS LEITNER

UNDERSTANDING GETHSEMANE

Gethsemane's reality, undoubtedly, has suffered much at the hands of both the artist and the theologian. The artist has dared to invest the scene with beauty when sorrow and horror should have been written large over all. The theologian has generally supplied elaborate explanations and interpretations when the simple narrative is so much more compelling and convincing than anything that can be said about it.

There is a better way than these for understanding Gethsemane, dark though its shadows may be. Let men hate sin as He hated it, let them love men as He loved them, let them dare to walk by faith even into the outer darkness for the sake of good to others. In these experiences Gethsemane shall be understood; its dark shadows shall flee away and, standing there, the eager soul shall see God waiting with outstretched hands of love.

GERHARD E. LENSKI

❖❖❖

HIDDEN LIGHT

"Where is the candle that I lit in thee?"
The Master cried.
I trembled at His side.
"It's hidden here, beneath this bushel, see?
I feared lest others know and laugh at me."
"You thought to hide
Within one bosom small
A gift intended for the good of all?"
His sad look pierced my heart,
And tore the selfish bushel wide apart.

ETHEL G. BEMIS

❖❖❖

Prayer is the greatest power that God has put into our hands for service. Prayer is harder work than doing, but in that way the Kingdom is advanced.

MARY SLESSOR

❖❖❖

SONG

What trees were in Gethsemane,
    What flowers were there to scent,
When Christ for you, and Christ for me,
    Into His garden went?

The fragrant cedar tree was there,
    The lily pale and slim;
They saw His grief, they heard His prayer,
    And wept their dews for Him.

And that is why the cedars green
    And why the lilies white
Do whisper of the Master's love
    In gardens, late at night.

CHARLES G. BLANDEN

❖❖❖

PURPOSE OF PRAYER

The purpose of prayer is not to change God's intention, which is already perfectly loving, but rather, by some mysterious process, which in our finiteness we cannot understand, to open channels of grace and power which otherwise are closed. If you can turn to God, at any time of day or night, as naturally and unpretentiously as a child turning to his mother, you have found the secret of the saints.

ELTON TRUEBLOOD

❖❖❖

CONVERGENCE

In prayer the highest and the lowest come together: the lowliest heart and the most exalted God.

JOHANN ARNDT

❖❖❖

JESUS PRAYING

He sought the mountain and the loneliest
        height,
    For He would meet His Father all alone,
And there, with many a tear and many a
        groan,
    He strove in prayer throughout the long,
        long night.

Why need He pray, who held by filial right,
    O'er all the world alike of thought and
        sense,
The fulness of His Sire's omnipotence?
    Why crave in prayer what was His own by
        might?
Vain is the question,—Christ was man in
        need,
    And being man His duty was to pray.

The Son of God confess'd the human need,
    And doubtless ask'd a blessing every day.
Nor ceases yet for sinful man to plead,
    Nor will, till heaven and earth shall pass
        away.

HARTLEY COLERIDGE

❖❖❖

It is not the arithmetic of our prayers,
  how many they are;
Nor the rhetoric of our prayers,
  how eloquent they may be;
Nor the geometry of our prayers,
  how long they may be;
Nor the logic of our prayers,
  how argumentative they may be;
Nor the method of our prayers,
  how orderly they may be;
It is the fervency of spirit which
  availeth much!

THE WESLEYAN METHODIST

❖❖❖

ON ENTERING A CHURCH

Come in
with love for God and man,
nor fear
to wait as stranger in this quiet place,
for God
Himself will presently appear
and smile a welcome from a friendly face
and offer you
with others waiting here,
the Bread of Fellowship
and the Cup of Grace.

EDWIN MC NEILL POTEAT

❖❖❖

Prayer is the simple interchange of thought
and feeling with God, rising out of conscious sensuousness into spirituality, turning one's self away from the things of time,
and standing upon the threshold of the
eternal world.

HENRY WARD BEECHER

❖❖❖

INWARD RESERVOIRS

Times of hush and meditation, "recollec-
tion" and integration, bring resources to life
as well as health and restoration. Serenity
comes not alone by removing the outward
causes and occasions of fear, but by the discovery of inward reservoirs of strength to
draw upon. There are deeps in us below the
level of our own thoughts and ideas. There
is a substratum in us that is the mother
soil of all our thinking and of all our doing,
out of which our ideas and ideals emerge,
"as capes of cloud out of the invisible air."
To feed, or to fertilize, this subsoil of our
lives is vastly more important than to pick
up and exploit a few more random ideas.

RUFUS M. JONES

❖❖❖

A SINGING HEART

Give me, dear God, a heart
  That bravely sings
When searing trials come,
  When joys take wings;
Teach me—before life's wan,
  Brief sun shall set—
That I can never scale
  Bright Olivet,
And from her crest look up
  Triumphantly,
Except I pass through dark
  Gethsemane!

WINNIE LYNCH ROCKETT

❖❖❖

Long ago the lilies faded which to Jesus
    seemed so fair,
  But the love that bade them blossom still
    is working everywhere.
In the fields and in the valleys, by the
    streams we love so well,
  There is greater glory blooming than the
    tongue of man can tell.

Long ago in sacred silence died the accents
    of His prayer;
  Still the souls that seek the Father find
    His presence everywhere.
Let us seek Him, still believing He that
    worketh round us yet,
  Clothing lilies in the meadows, will His
    children ne'er forget.

WILLIAM G. TARRANT

CHANNEL

A Christian is a mind through which Christ
thinks;
a heart through which Christ loves;
a voice through which Christ speaks;
a hand through which Christ helps.

GEORGE MUELLER

NATURE OF PRAYER

Once we grasp the true nature of prayer, the
difficulties which are so often urged against
the practice of intercession are seen to be
entirely irrelevant.

Knowing all human life to be one; knowing ourselves to be vitally and indissolubly
knit to our brethren in God, knowing that
He sees mankind as living in relations of
mutual interdependence, united by their
common response to eternal love, intercession becomes a vital necessity.

We see our mutual interdependence
broken, because of the failure of so many to
respond to the love of God and take their
place in His family; and the love of Christ
constrains us to take His way of self-oblation
on their behalf.

EMILY HERMAN

BEATITUDES OF A LEADER

Blessed is the leader who has not sought the
high places but who has been drafted into
service because of his ability and willingness to serve.

Blessed is the leader who knows where
he is going, why he is going, and how to
get there.

Blessed is the leader who knows no discouragement, who presents no alibi.

Blessed is the leader who knows how
to lead without being dictatorial, for true
leaders are humble.

Blessed is the leader who seeks for the
best for those he serves.

Blessed is the leader who leads for the
good of the most concerned and not for
the personal gratification of his own ideas.

Blessed is the leader who develops leaders
while leading.

Blessed is the leader who marches with
the group and interprets correctly the signs
on the pathway that leads to success.

Blessed is the leader who has his head
in the clouds but his feet on the ground.

MOOD OF ASPIRATION

Worship is not primarily a mode of
expression. It is primarily a mood of aspiration.

It is not primarily a way of doing something. It is primarily a feeling of desire to do
that thing.

Those who forget or overlook this fact
are the formalists, the ritualists, the play-
actors of religion. They have lost their way.

He who is so greatly concerned about
mode that he neglects the cultivation of
mood is like a man who lays out a garden
in the desert sands without having first assured himself that there are springs of water
in the hills which may be diverted and
caused to fertilize the soil.

DWIGHT BRADLEY

HIS PEACE

I love to think of them at dawn
    Beneath the frail pink sky
Casting their nets in Galilee
    And fish-hawks circling by.

Casting their nets in Galilee
    Just off the hills of brown,
Such happy, simple fisherfolk
    Before the Lord walked down.

Contented, peaceful fishermen,
    Before they ever knew

The peace of God that filled their hearts
  Brim-full, and broke them too.

Young John who trimmed the flapping sail,
  Homeless, in Patmos died.
Peter who hauled the teeming net,
  Head-down, was crucified.

The peace of God, it is no peace,
  But strife closed in the sod.
Yet, brothers, pray for but one thing,
  The marvellous peace of God.

WILLIAM ALEXANDER PERCY

❖❖❖

INFLUENCE

The least may influence the greatest.

It was St. Andrew that influenced St. Peter to "come and see" Jesus. One least spoken of among the apostles influenced the one who took the foremost place among them as if to show that such power is independent of personal superiority.

It is not the great and gifted alone who exercise this mysterious power of influence. It is a universal law of life.

These personal influences, first of Jesus on Andrew, then of Andrew on Peter, were the beginning of the conversion of the world.

T. T. CARTER

❖❖❖

WHAT IS CHRISTIANITY?

To examine its evidence is not to try Christianity; to admire its martyrs is not to try Christianity; to compare and estimate its teachers is not to try Christianity; to attend its rites and services is not to try or know Christianity. But for one week, for one day, to have lived in the pure atmosphere of faith and love to God, of tenderness to man; to have beheld earth annihilated, and heaven opened to the prophetic gaze of hope; to have seen evermore revealed behind the complicated troubles of this strange, mysterious life, the unchanged smile of an eternal Friend, and everything that is difficult to reason solved by that reposing trust which is higher and better than reason—to have known and felt this, I will not say for a life, but for a single blessed hour, that, indeed, is to have made experiment of Christianity.

WILLIAM ARCHER BUTLER

❖❖❖

THIRTY-THREE YEARS

How young He was, how short His time
  on earth!
  A pulse-beat through the centuries, a
  breath
Between the starlit hour of His birth
  And that strange darkened hour of His
  death!

Yet had those years not gone their swift sure
  way,
  Had their significance been lost to men,
There would be darkness in the land today,
  No faith would lift, no heart could hope
  again.

Thank God, thank God for those years'
  precious store!
  Thank God for sparing Him to you, to
  me,
"Out of the glory that was theirs before
  The world was . . ." and the glory yet to
  be.

The darkened years for Him, that brought
  us light;
  The weary years for Him, that gave us
  rest;
The clamorous years, that we might know
  the white
  High silences of peace within the breast.

For thirty-three brief years that His feet trod
  The earthly roads for us, we thank Thee,
  God.

GRACE NOLL CROWELL

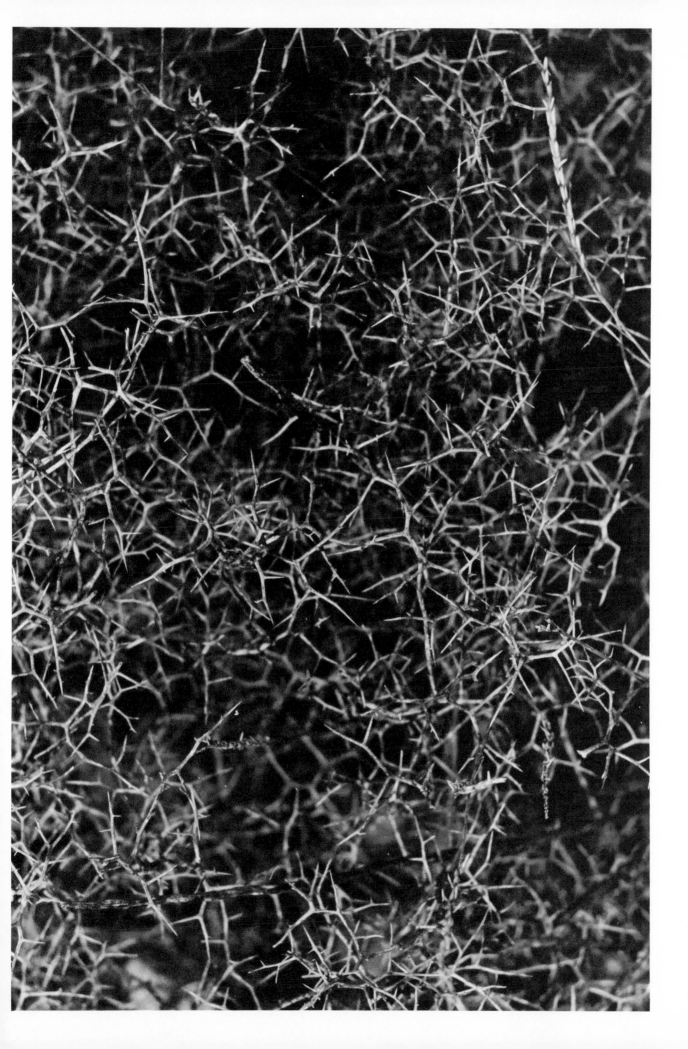

SOCIETY OF SINNERS

The glory of the Church, its uniqueness, is that it lives perpetually on the vitality and realism of its own repentance, its contrition, and its plea for God's help and forgiveness.

Let us not claim moral virtue for church members or for the Church.

Let us rather glory in the fact that the Church is a society of sinners who claim no virtue but humbly rest their broken and burdened lives upon the grace which God has eternally revealed in Christ Jesus.

CHARLES CLAYTON MORRISON

GARDENS AND GARDENERS

The inner life or soul of man is like a garden, which, if carefully and wisely tended, yields both flowers and fruit.

If neglected it may quickly become a wilderness of weeds, unsightly and unproductive, a danger moreover to other gardens.

Each of us is not only garden but gardener, and it is not only the powers of nature, but we, who control the issue. Response to a gardener's care has both inward and outward aspects.

There are the hidden processes by which roots and leaves absorb food material from soil and air, and make it part of the plant's own substance.

There are the more external but still mysterious processes by which colorless sap is transformed into beauty of flower and richness of fruit.

So, in the soul's garden, the outer life of conduct and service depends on a healthy inner life of spiritual assimilation.

The chief conditions of such assimilation are prayer and meditation, together with an attitude of receptivity: what Wordsworth calls "feeding this mind of ours in a wise passiveness."

EDWARD GRUBB

Prayer is love melted into worship.

CHARLES H. BRENT

A PRAYER

Dear Father, now a day has come and gone,
And brought what things a day may hold of care
And ease and toil, of courage, of despair
For sins not conquered and the race not won.
And now an hour with Thee to look upon
The day in retrospect, to weave a prayer
From broken strands of thought. I am aware
Of guilt that steals from me Thy benison.
But peace shall come; before the veil that hides
Thy face, a fragrant incense rises still
In symbol of a life of sinlessness.
My failures vanish; in their place abides
His triumph. My indifference, gray and chill,
Is warmed by deeds of love in Nazareth.

MARYAN B. WILKINSON

Mount
of the Beatitudes

. . . and He taught them

LEARNING

❖❖❖

SCRIPTURE

Train up a child in the way he should go: and when he is old, he will not depart from it.

PROVERBS 22:6

For whatsoever things were written aforetime were written for our learning, that we through patience and comfort of the scriptures might have hope.

ROMANS 15:4

And seeing the multitudes, he went up into a mountain: and when he was set, his disciples came unto him: and he opened his mouth, and taught them, saying, Blessed are the poor in spirit: for theirs is the kingdom of heaven. Blessed are they that mourn: for they shall be comforted. Blessed are the meek: for they shall inherit the earth. Blessed are they which do hunger and thirst after righteousness: for they shall be filled. Blessed are the merciful: for they shall obtain mercy. Blessed are the pure in heart: for they shall see God. Blessed are the peacemakers: for they shall be called the children of God. Blessed are they which are persecuted for righteousness' sake: for theirs is the kingdom of heaven. Blessed are ye, when men shall revile you, and persecute you, and shall say all manner of evil against you falsely, for my sake. Rejoice, and be exceeding glad: for great is your reward in heaven.

MATTHEW 5:1–12

❖❖❖

MEDITATION

The "Horns of Hattin," a twin-peaked hill overlooking the Sea of Galilee on the road from Tiberias to Nazareth, was said by the Crusaders to be the Mount of the Beatitudes where Jesus spoke the imperishable words found in the Sermon on the Mount.

Hattin is a second Mount Sinai, except that here the way and will of God were measured not by the yardstick of the Law but by the compulsions of love.

Through the centuries unnumbered multitudes have found in these words a summary of Jesus' instructions and counsel concerning righteousness and have been inspired by the Beatitudes, which are His guideposts to blessedness and spiritual joy.

As we listen to the world's Schoolmaster, who speaks in an informal and personal manner, we recognize that what He says is eternally relevant and pointedly contemporary.

We too discern, as did our spiritual forefathers, that He is "a teacher come from God" who speaks as "one having authority." His lessons have been the single most decisive influence in the intellectual and moral life of man, and today His classroom is world-wide.

69

THE MOUNT OF THE BEATITUDES

It was a little mountain, with no name
  For overwhelming altitudes, no claim
To being earth's most majestic, most sub-
    lime;
  It was a mountain weary folk could climb.
And on the lowly mountain small winds
    went
  Sighing across the grasses meekly bent
Beneath the weight of many trampling feet,
  And sparrows twittered, finding seeds to
    eat
In merciful supply, beneath the pure
  Blue sky, and home trees peacefully se-
    cure.

And here the searching people heard Him
    speak
  His blessing on the humble, mournful,
    meek,
The needy, merciful, and pure, and all
  Peacemakers, and those whom men mis-
    treat, and call
Hard names for living thus. The startling
    words,
  Mingled with chirps of confident small
    birds,
Brought guilty consternation and disdain
  To many, and to others wistful pain,
But many hearers, eagerly receiving,
  Found joy beyond belief in sure be-
    lieving.

No inaccessibility excludes
  Us from the Mount of the Beatitudes.
If we but firmly, finally put aside
  Our anxious selfish righteousness and
    pride
And strive in earnest love to do His will,
  Our hearts may hear Him saying,
    "Blessed," still.

JANE MERCHANT

THE WAY

The Scriptures teach us the best way of
living, the noblest way of suffering, and
the most comfortable way of dying.

JOHN FLAVEL

LIFE IN MINIATURE

The Sermon on the Mount is the Christian
way of life in miniature. No other piece
of literature of like length has such far-
reaching implications for the transforming
of the human race. Given this message in
three chapters of Matthew, plus the life,
death, and resurrection of Jesus who gave
the message, you have enough to save our
civilization or any other if it can be accepted.

ARLO AYRES BROWN

IMMORTAL WORDS

Above the Lake of Galilee
  Soft winds are blowing still,
With lyric words of love set free
  Above the Lake of Galilee.

They blow across the timeless sea,
  Immortal words that thrill.
Above the Lake of Galilee
  Soft winds are blowing still.

ALINE BADGER CARTER

CHRIST'S BIOGRAPHY

The Sermon on the Mount is Christ's biog-
raphy. Every syllable He had already written down in deeds. The sermon merely
translated His life into language.

THOMAS WRIGHT

70

It takes only fifteen minutes to read the greatest sermon ever preached—and when you have finished it, you will have read a complete summary of all that Jesus taught.

CHARLES L. ALLEN

❖❖❖

THE EDUCATION OF JESUS

The Gospels record not only the final examination to which He was subjected at the end of His schooling, but the actual response He made to such a test.

It took place, as you will remember, on an isolated mountain-top at the very beginning of His ministry and commonly we speak of it as His temptation.

Here He showed unmistakably that, indifferent though His training was from our point of view, He had acquired from it certain convictions and attitudes without which the noblest education may well be a futility.

He knew His way to an invisible source of strength on which He could draw in any emergency.

He had learned to distinguish between ephemeral and lasting values. He was schooled in selflessness.

He had acquired a sense of responsibility which gave to His life a clear-cut purpose.

He has been rubbed free from petty racial and social prejudice until He could see the world in terms of humanity.

All this rings through His words and shines from His face, when we see Him there on the mountain-top during His hour of ordeal, robust and vigorous in His young manhood, as He squares Himself to face His task in the world.

CARL HOPKINS ELMORE

❖❖❖

Thou art sought, and thou seekest. As thou dealest with *thy* seeker, even so will God deal with *His*. Thou art both empty and full. Fill thou the empty out of thy fulness,

that out of the fulness of God thine emptiness may be filled.

ST. AUGUSTINE

❖❖❖

He spake of lilies, vines and corn,
The sparrow and the raven,
And the words so natural yet so wise
Were on men's hearts engraven.

And yeast and bread and flax and cloth
And eggs and fish and candles.
See how the most familiar world
He most divinely handles.

GEORGE A. BARTON

❖❖❖

The whole teaching of Jesus Christ about God, expressed alike in His words and in the whole fashion and mould of His character, implies that God is always nearer, mightier, more loving, and more free to help every one of us than any one of us ever realizes.

D. S. CAIRNS

❖❖❖

JESUS AND YOUTH

Jesus was devoted to youth. His most beloved disciple was the youngest of the twelve. The ideal He held up before all of His followers was that of a heart perpetually young. Of such, He said, is the kingdom of heaven.

One of the most scathing judgments which fell from His lips was upon the man who put a stumbling block in the path of youth. "Whoever is a hindrance to any one of these little ones who believe in me, it were better for him to have a great millstone hung about his neck and be sunk in the sea." That statement seems to have made a profound impression upon the friends of Jesus, for it is recorded in all three of the Synoptic Gospels.

Reading these words we must be aware that if Jesus were here today He would be concerned in what is happening to our youth.

ALBERT EDWARD DAY

❖❖❖

UNSURPASSED

Jesus of Nazareth is unsurpassed in the field of religious poetry, unsurpassed in the brilliance of His dialectic, unsurpassed in His capacity to express profound truth in simple language, supreme in the expression of an ultimate moral standard, and remarkable for the supreme mastery over life which is manifest in the records of His career.

STEPHEN NEILL

❖❖❖

MASTER BUILDER

Only the Hands of Nazareth
  Could have used such knotted wood
As the lives of Peter, Thomas, the Twelve,
  For building a base that stood
When palaces of Caesar fell,
  For laying foundations broad
As love itself, that outlast time
  For the carpentry of God.

LESLIE SAVAGE CLARK

❖❖❖

From WE WOULD SEE JESUS

We would see Jesus, on the mountain teaching,
  With all the listening people gathered round;
While birds and flowers and sky above are preaching,
  The blessedness which simple trust has found.

We would see Jesus, in His work of healing,
  At the eventide before the sun was set;
Divine and human, in His deep revealing,
  Of God and man in loving service met.

JOHN EDGAR PARK

❖❖❖

INSCRIPTION

Man's ultimate destiny depends not on whether he can learn new lessons or make new discoveries and conquests, but on his acceptance of the lesson taught him close upon two thousand years ago.

ROCKEFELLER CENTER

❖❖❖

PSALM

The Lord is my teacher.
  I shall not want.
  He maketh me to learn in God's out-of-doors.
  He teacheth me by His written word. He instructeth my soul.
  He guideth me in the paths of true knowledge for His name's sake.
  Yea, when the day's task is done, and life's lessons have been learned, I will fear no evil, for Thou wilt be with me, my Teacher and my Comforter still.
  Thou teachest even my enemies to become pupils of the Great Teacher.
  Thou leadest me gently from the known to the unknown.
  Thou givest me satisfaction in my day's work.
  Surely goodness and mercy shall follow me all the days of my life, and I shall be a learner in the school of the Great Teacher forever.

FREDERIC S. GOODRICH

❖❖❖

THE SISTERS

The waves forever move;
  The hills forever rest:
Yet each the heavens approve,
  And Love alike hath blessed
A Martha's household care,
  A Mary's cloistered prayer.

JOHN BANISTER TABB

THE BIBLE

This book contains the mind of God, the state of man, the way of salvation, the doom of sinners, and the happiness of believers.

Its doctrines are holy, its precepts are binding, its histories are true, and its decisions are immutable.

Read it to be wise, believe it to be safe, and practice it to be holy.

It contains light to direct you, food to support you, and comfort to cheer you.

It is the traveler's map, the pilgrim's staff, the soldier's sword, and the Christian's charter.

Here paradise is restored, heaven opened, and the gates of hell disclosed. Christ is its grand object, our good its design, and the glory of God its end.

It should fill the memory, rule the heart, and guide the feet.

Read it slowly, frequently and prayerfully.

It is a mine of wealth, a paradise of glory, and a river of pleasure.

It is given you in life, will be opened in the judgment, and be remembered forever.

It involves the highest responsibility, will reward the greatest labor, and will condemn all who trifle with its sacred content.

❖❖❖

SPOKEN TRUTHS AND SPIRIT INCARNATE

Jesus originated no series of well-concerted plans; He neither contrived nor put in motion any extended machinery; He entered into no correspondence with parties in His own country and in other regions of the world, in order to spread His influence and obtain cooperation.

Even the few who were His constant companions, and were warmly attached to His person, were not, in His lifetime, imbued with His sentiments, and were not prepared to take up His work in His spirit after He was gone.

He constituted no society with its name, design, and laws all definitely fixed and formally established.

He had no time to construct and to organize—His life was too short—and almost all He did was to speak.

He spoke in familiar conversation with His friends, or at the wayside to passersby, or to those who chose to consult Him, or to large assemblies as opportunity offered.

He left behind Him a few spoken truths—not a line or word of writing—and a certain spirit incarnated in His principles and breathed out from His life; and then He died.

JOHN YOUNG

❖❖❖

I HOLD THE BOOK

Here in my hands I hold the Holy Book.
  Like silence coming after battle roar,
So peace comes home, and all the storms that shook
  The heart's foundation are no more, no more.
Now unafraid, I watch the level length
  Of shadows deepen into darkest night:
Here in my hands is quietness and strength,
  Here in my hands is gentleness and might.

Though satellites may whirl in outer space,
  And hearts may faint with fear, this heart of mine
Is confident. I hold the Book and trace
  God's faithfulness in every single line.
And though the midnight of the world be nearing,
  I face the dawn, the day of His appearing.

HELEN FRAZEE-BOWER

❖❖❖

74

THE MAN OF GALILEE

He was no dreamer, dwelling in a cloud
    Of idle reason, strange philosophy;
In simple tasks His manhood strong He
      bowed
    Beneath hard toil and meagre poverty.
Simple, not strange, the living words He
      saith—
    The toiling Carpenter of Nazareth.

I cannot find Him, when, with fertile brain
    I ponder strange, amazing mystery;
But when my heart is darkened by the pain
    Of weariness or doubt or misery,
And someone smiles or haply calls me
      friend,
    Or does a duty self-effacingly,
'Tis then His glowing face doth seem to
      bend
    Above me, and the living Christ I see—
The Son of God, the Man of Galilee.

               HILDEGARDE HOYT SWIFT

❖❖❖

BLESSEDNESS

The world has its own idea of blessedness. Blessed is the man who is always right. Blessed is the man who is satisfied with himself. Blessed is the man who is strong. Blessed is the man who rules. Blessed is the man who is rich. Blessed is the man who is popular. Blessed is the man who enjoys life. These are the beatitudes of sight and of this present world.

It comes with a shock and opens a new realm of thought, that not one of these men entered Jesus' mind when He treated of blessedness. "Blessed," said Jesus, "is the man who thinks lowly of himself; who has passed through great trials; who gives in and endures; who longs for perfection; who carries a tender heart; who has a passion for holiness; who sweetens human life; who dares to be true to conscience."

What a conception of character! For the first time a halo rests on gentleness, patience, kindness, and sanctity, and the eight men of the Beatitudes divide the Kingdom of God.

               JOHN WATSON

❖❖❖

AS HE WALKED WITH US

Calm, strong, and gentle Man of Galilee,
    Whose heart by every human voice is
      stirred;
    By whom are plaintive cries of creatures
      heard;
Whose eye escapes no tracery of tree,
Or modest wayside flower; alert to see
    The fantasy of cloud, the flight of bird;
    Whose ear can catch the faintest note and
      word
Of wind and stream, and distant western
      sea;
When I am treading on the open space,
    Or threading slowly through the crowded
      marts,
Skilled Craftsman of the woods and market
      place,
    Companion of all life and human hearts,
I crave, Thou unseen, understanding
      Guide,
To find Thee, silent, walking by my side.

          HARRY WEBB FARRINGTON

❖❖❖

ONE THERE WAS

One there was who, passing by,
    Touched all life with alchemy,
Grass of field or birds of air
    Made His heart of God aware
Of common salt or smooth-worn yoke
    A figure patterned for eager folk;
Of wayside spring or granary
    Symbols He made which never die;
From mustard seed or branching vine,
    Similitudes of things divine.
Meaning to leavening dough He lent;
    He made, of bread, a sacrament.

          STELLA FISHER BURGESS

❖❖❖

Grant me, O Lord,
to know that which is worth knowing,
to love that which is worth loving,
to praise that which pleaseth Thee most,
to esteem that which is most precious unto
    Thee,
to dislike whatever is evil in Thy eyes,
and to search out and to do what is well-
    pleasing unto Thee.

THOMAS A KEMPIS

❖❖❖

A YOUTH MOVEMENT

He selected twelve young men between the
approximate ages of eighteen and thirty.

They had time, resiliency, stamina, and
capacity.

They were not bound by the routine responsibilities of homes and organizations.

They were not restricted by the fixed
prejudices and provincial loyalties so common to old age.

None was hindered by priestly or political ties or aspirations.

Their capacity for God had not been
crystallized.

They were teachable.

They were able to see the issues of life.

They were able to hear the still, sad music
of humanity.

They were able to feel indignation and
kindness.

They were able to recognize truth and
submit themselves to its obligations.

They were able to grow in wisdom concerning God and man.

A. C. REID

❖❖❖

From THE WORD

Voice of the Holy Spirit, making known
    Man to himself, a witness swift and sure,
Warning, approving, true and wise and
    pure,

Counsel and guidance that misleadeth
    none!
By Thee the mystery of life is read;
    The picture-writing of the world's gray
        seers,
The myths and parables of the primal years,
    Whose letter kills, by Thee interpreted
Take healthful meanings fitted to our
    needs,
    And in the soul's vernacular express
The common law of simple righteousness.
    Hatred of cant and doubt and human
        creeds
May well be felt; the unpardonable sin
    Is to deny the Word of God within!

JOHN GREENLEAF WHITTIER

❖❖❖

All a child's life depends on the ideal it
has of its parents. Destroy that and everything goes—morals, behavior, everything.
Absolute trust in someone else is the essence
of education.

E. M. FORSTER

❖❖❖

CONTEMPLATION UPON FLOWERS

Brave flowers, that I could gallant it like
    you,
    And be as little vain!
You come abroad, and make a harmless
    show,
    And to your beds of earth again.
You are not proud; you know your birth;
For your embroidered garments are from
    earth.

You do obey your months and times, but I
    Would have it ever Spring.
My fate would know no Winter, never die,
    Nor think of such a thing.
O that I could my bed of earth but view
And smile, and look as cheerfully as you!

HENRY KING

Bethlehem

. . . for unto us a Child is born

CHRISTMAS

❖❖❖

SCRIPTURE

The people that walked in darkness have seen a great light: they that dwell in the land of the shadow of death, upon them hath the light shined. . . . For unto us a child is born, unto us a son is given: and the government shall be upon his shoulder: and his name shall be called Wonderful, Counsellor, The mighty God, The everlasting Father, The Prince of Peace.

ISAIAH 9:2, 6

And thou Bethlehem, in the land of Juda, art not the least among the princes of Juda: for out of thee shall come a Governor, that shall rule my people Israel. . . . Behold, a virgin shall be with child, and shall bring forth a son, and they shall call his name Emmanuel, which being interpreted is, God with us.

MATTHEW 2:6; 1:23

And suddenly there was with the angel a multitude of the heavenly host praising God, and saying, Glory to God in the highest, and on earth peace, good will toward men.

LUKE 2:13–14

In him was life; and the life was the light of men. And the light shineth in darkness; and the darkness comprehended it not.

JOHN 1:4–5

❖❖❖

MEDITATION

Twenty-seven centuries ago Micah wrote, "But thou, Bethlehem Ephratah, though thou be little among the thousands of Judah, yet out of thee shall he come forth unto me that is to be ruler in Israel."

This prophecy came to pass when, in the fullness of time, the Messiah was born in the storied town where Jacob had buried his beloved Rachel, Boaz had wed Ruth, and David had been anointed by Samuel.

Bethlehem, which has engraved Christmas on the heart of humanity, is situated on the eastern side of a limestone ridge five miles south of Jerusalem. On a clear day a pilgrim in the Holy Land can look from the fields where angels sang to shepherds to the city where the Son of God "for the joy that was set before him endured the cross, despising the shame."

On Christmas today in the City of David a Christian seems to hear the footsteps of the Wise Men from the East and to feel the heartthrob of the Virgin Mother who said, "Behold the handmaid of the Lord; be it unto me according to thy word." Here are met "the hopes and fears of all the years," for "the hinge of history is on the door of a Bethlehem stable."

HOW FAR TO BETHLEHEM?

"How far is it to Bethlehem town?"
  Just over the Jerusalem hills adown,
Past lovely Rachel's white-domed tomb—
  Sweet shrine of motherhood's young
    doom.

It isn't far to Bethlehem town—
  Just over the dusty roads adown,
Past Wise Men's well, still offering
  Cool draughts from welcome wayside
    spring;
Past shepherds with their flutes of reed
  That charm the woolly sheep they lead;
Past boys with kites on hill-tops flying,
  And soon you're there where Bethlehem's
    lying,
Sunned white and sweet on olived slopes,
  Gold-lighted still with Judah's hopes.

And so we find the Shepherd's field
  The plain that gave rich Boaz yield;
And look where Herod's villa stood.
  We thrill that earthly parenthood
Could foster Christ who was all-good;
  And thrill that Bethlehem town today
Looks down on Christian homes that pray.
  It isn't far to Bethlehem town!
It's anywhere that Christ comes down
  And finds in people's friendly face
A welcome and abiding place.
  The road to Bethlehem runs right
    through
The homes of folks like me and you.

MADELEINE SWEENY MILLER

❖❖❖

REVELATION

The feet of the humblest may walk in the
    fields
  Where the feet of the holiest have trod.
This, this is the marvel to mortals revealed,
  That mankind are the children of God.

PHILLIPS BROOKS

THE UNVEILING OF GOD

The advent of Jesus is more than a date—
it is an event; not simply an incident, but an
era: it is the unveiling of God and humanity. The long periods—B.C. and A.D.—are the
"folding doors of history," when prophecy
was fulfilled. The time and place and persons involved in this story are all of deep
significance to us, and the question that the
wise men came asking, "Where is He?" is
the deepest question of the ages.

S. STEPHEN MCKENNEY

❖❖❖

CHRISTMAS GIFTS

God gave His Son the softness of a dove;
Some shepherds gave the little Lamb their
  love;

A wise man gave the infant King his myrrh,
While Mary gave her Jesus all of her.

Good Joseph gave his Boy a trade to ply;
And we?—a Tree, twisted, on which to die.

JOHNSTONE G. PATRICK

❖❖❖

HILLS OF BETHLEHEM

O hills of Bethlehem that slept
  All through that shadowed night
Unheeding of the miracle
  That shone with holy light.

O hills of Bethlehem that woke
  When angel harps were playing,
And blossomed forth in ecstasy
  No beauty then delaying.

O hills of Bethlehem that keep
  Those memories divine,
The birth of Christ and Galilee
  Have made of you a shrine.

ANNE MURRY MOVIUS

✦✦✦

Bethlehem is the Greenwich from which all longitude of time is reckoned.

ELMER ELLSWORTH HELMS

✦✦✦

GEOGRAPHY OF JESUS

Let the land I know be the land He roves—
  My peach orchards stand for olive groves,
And lakes too cool for Galilee
  Be found in His geography.

Under its neon diadem
  Let my town be His Bethlehem;
But most of all, may I be able
  To let my heart become His stable.

RALPH W. SEAGER

✦✦✦

HOW GOD COMES

Two weary travelers enter the village on a night that can scarcely be distinguished from a thousand other nights. Bureaucracy must have more tax moneys! And a Child is born. A Child. Not Athena sprung fully grown and fully armored from the head of Zeus. Not a resplendent king descending in a flaming chariot from the heavens. Only a birth, the most common of human experiences. This is how God comes.

One would have expected the burst of a meteor, a brilliant sun at midnight, a burning bush, a pillar and a cloud, a parting of the waters. But none of these things happens. A Child is born at the hour of twelve, so pious legend tells us, to a mother of humble origin. We should have thought God would have chosen dawn when the heavens are aglow with the variegated colors of the rising sun, or twilight when the hand of day reaches high to pull down the purple curtains of the night. How strange are the ways of God!

Yet the very ordinariness of that first Christmas pleads knowingly and persuasively to common people. Christmas came to little Bethlehem that we might know that no place is unknown to God; at the stroke of twelve to remind us that there is no moment of the day or night when He is absent from us; to young Mary to convince us that all life is dear to Him; and in a Child that we may sense all of life is in His hands. Christmas is His monogram, stenciled on our hearts, recalling to us year by year that "no more is God a Stranger."

CHARLES L. WALLIS

✦✦✦

BETHLEHEM'S STALL

The creatures there in Bethlehem's stall
  Who looked upon the Christ-Child small—
I wonder if they knew at all

That someday His skilled hands would form
  An easy yoke; a stable warm
To shelter them from wind and storm;

That o'er His head a dove's white wing
  Would make the heavenly choirs to sing
That God was pleased His Son to bring;

That He would choose an ass's foal
  To ride upon, in kingly role
To claim the Kingdom of the Soul.

The little Lamb of God was He
  Who lay there sleeping silently,
The Shepherd of us all to be.

The creatures there within the stall
  Looked down upon that Baby small—
I wonder if they knew at all!

JILL MORGAN

✦✦✦

Christmas returns, as it always does, with its assurance that life is good.

It is the time of life to the spirit, when the mind feels its way into the common place and senses the wonder of simple things: an evergreen tree, familiar carols, merry laughter.

It is the time of illumination, when candles burn and old dreams find their youth again.

It is the time to pause, when forgotten joys come back to mind and past dedications renew their claim.

It is the time of harvest for the heart, when faith reaches out to mantle all high endeavor and love whispers its magic word to everything that breathes.

HOWARD THURMAN

❖❖❖

BIRTH OF HOPE

The darkest night is not without its star.
The hopeless hours are oft before the dawn.
The travail and pangs of life's long years must come before eternal hope is born.

SUNSHINE MAGAZINE

❖❖❖

Christmas is a little child with wonder in his eyes.

GEORGE L. WHITLOCK

❖❖❖

CHRISTMAS PRAYER

O God, who scarfs this Christmas world
    with snow
And lights star tapers so that all may see,
Please leave beneath the tinseled pine's
    clear glow
    Your gifts of faith, love, peace, and
    charity.

MARIAN PAUST

❖❖❖

KINGS AND STARS

As they came from the East
    Following a star,

One said:
    The sun burns,
The moon changes,
    Stars are faithful.

One said:
    They shine in all tongues,
Every heart knows them,
    By starlight there are no borders.

One said:
    The world widens
By starlight,
    The mind reaches;
Stars beget journeys.

JOHN ERSKINE

❖❖❖

BENEDICTION

God grant you the light in Christmas, which is faith.

The warmth of Christmas, which is love.

The radiance of Christmas, which is purity.

The righteousness of Christmas, which is justice.

The belief in Christmas, which is truth.

The all of Christmas, which is Christ.

WILDA ENGLISH

❖❖❖

O LEST WE STARVE

O lest we starve, and lest we die
    In our stupidity,
Come, Holy Child, within and share
    Our hospitality.

RALPH SPAULDING CUSHMAN

❖❖❖

GOD MUST HAVE KNOWN

The angels came and set a star one night
　To mark a shining path to Bethlehem;
And having placed it in the diadem
　Of silver worlds, they took their silver
　　flight
To bare, brown fields where shepherds saw
　　the bright
　Full glory of the Lord revealed to them,
And heard a song of joy; the hills that hem
　The plains rang angel music from their
　　height.
These simple shepherds heard the angels'
　　song
　And held it in their hearts the while
　　they ran
The starry path of faith to own the Christ;
　God must have known these humble
　　men would long
To tell the world His love and peace could
　　span
　All time, they would fulfill their angel
　　tryst.

RUTH B. VAN DEUSEN

❖❖❖

RELEVANCE

The most amazing thing of all about the
Christmas story is its relevance.

　It is at home in every age and fits into
every mood of life.

　It is not simply a lovely tale once told,
but eternally contemporary.

　It is the voice crying in every wilderness.

　It is as meaningful in our time as in
that long ago night when shepherds followed the light of the star to the manger
of Bethlehem.

JOSEPH R. SIZOO

❖❖❖

THE CHRISTMAS VISION

What would it mean to live by the vision
which comes on Christmas Eve?

It would mean to trust God and not
give way to worry and faithless fears.

　It would mean to act on the faith that
the supreme power in the universe is the
love of God seeking good for all men
everywhere.

　It would mean to practice love in daily
life, at home and in every human relationship.

ERNEST FREMONT TITTLE

❖❖❖

WISE MEN SEEKING JESUS

Wise men seeking Jesus
　Traveled from afar,
Guided on their journey
　By a beauteous star.
But if we desire Him,
　He is close at hand;
For our native country
　Is our Holy Land.

Prayerful souls may find Him
　By our quiet lakes,
Meet Him on our hillsides
　Where the morning breaks.
In our fertile cornfields,
　While the sheaves are bound,
In our busy markets
　Jesus may be found.

Every peaceful village
　In our land might be,
Made by Jesus' presence
　Like sweet Bethany.
He is more than near us,
　If we love Him well;
For He seeketh ever
　In our hearts to dwell.

JAMES EAST

❖❖❖

THE ART OF KEEPING CHRISTMAS

How can we best keep Christmas? How can we best defeat the little bit of Scrooge in all of us and experience the glory of the Great Day?

By sinking the shafts of our spirits deep beneath the sparkling tinsel of the surface of Christmas and renewing within us the radiance of the inner meaning of the season.

By following the Star on an inward journey to Bethlehem to stand again in awe and wonder before the Babe in a Manger.

By rediscovering the faith and simplicity of a little child, for of such is the Kingdom of Heaven.

By being still and listening to the angels sing within our hearts.

By quietly evaluating our lives according to the Master's standards as set forth in the Sermon on the Mount.

By reaffirming the supremacy of the spirit in man's conquest of himself.

By rededicating ourselves to the Master's ideals of Peace, Brotherhood and Good Will.

By resolving to give ourselves away to others in love, joy and devotion.

By using the light of Christmas to guide us through the darkness of the coming year, refusing to go back to the dim kerosene lamps of the spirit when the brilliant electricity of Christmas is available to show us the way.

WILFERD A. PETERSON

❖❖❖

'Tis not enough that Christ was born
  Beneath the star that shone,
And earth was set that holy morn
  Within a golden zone.
He must be born within the heart,
  Before He finds His throne,
And brings the day of love and good,
  The reign of Christ-like brotherhood.

MARY T. LATHROP

❖❖❖

NEVER NIGHT AGAIN

The soft light from a stable door
  Lies on the midnight lands.
The Wise Men's star burns evermore
  Over all desert sands.

Unto all peoples of the earth
  A little Child brought light,
And never in the darkest place
  Can it be utter night.

No flickering torch, no wavering fire,
  But Light—the Life of men.
Whatever clouds may veil the sky,
  Never is night again!

LILIAN COX

❖❖❖

The road to Bethlehem leads home again, that we may show there what great things God has done for us.

ARTHUR LICHTENBERGER

❖❖❖

ALWAYS A STAR

There's always a Star,
  If the eyes wish to see;
For the wise travel far,
  When their vision is free.

There's always a Child
  In a manger so bare,
But the angels of God
  Stand guarding Him there.

Wise men of today
  From near and afar
Seek light through the Child
  In the peace of the Star.

GILBERT DARLINGTON

❖❖❖

DECEMBER TWENTY-FOURTH

Tomorrow You are born again
  Who died so many times.
Do You like the candle-light,
  Do You like the chimes?

Do You stop to wonder
  Why men never see
How very closely Bethlehem
  Approaches Calvary?

ELEANOR SLATER

✥✥✥

PERSISTENT INFLUENCE

When Mary's Child was born there in the stable on a winter's night, with no warmth to give her comfort except the warmth that came from the bodies of asses and of oxen lying near, the vast indifference of the Roman world, unknowing and unconcerned, seemed to smother that event in Bethlehem with all the weight of its remote contempt.

What did it matter to Caesar that a peasant mother in one of the far-off provinces held a Baby in her arms that night? What contemptuous laughter would have rung from the lips of Roman legionaries if it had been suggested that there in the Child's life was a power more enduring and more irresistible than their swords. To the calculations of the world the fact of the Child Jesus would have seemed a thing utterly devoid of consequence.

Yet the personality of Jesus so transfigured those facts of His existence that He remains today as the one great influence from those ancient years which reaches across the centuries with an immortal power. Caesar Augustus and all the glory of his empire are gone, and the long-vanished centuries are the winding-sheet in which the dead glories of Rome have descended into the dust.

WALTER RUSSELL BOWIE

✥✥✥

THE CHRISTMAS SPIRIT

I am the Christmas Spirit!

I enter the home of poverty, causing pale-faced children to open their eyes wide in pleased wonder.

I cause the miser's clutched hand to relax, and thus paint a bright spot in his soul.

I cause the aged to renew their youth and to laugh in the old, glad way.

I keep romance alive in the heart of childhood, and brighten sleep with dreams woven of magic.

I cause eager feet to climb dark stairways with filled baskets, leaving behind hearts amazed at the goodness of the world.

I cause the prodigal to pause a moment on his wild, wasteful way, and send to anxious love some little token that releases glad tears—tears which wash away the hard lines of sorrow.

I enter dark prison cells, reminding scarred manhood of what might have been, and pointing forward to good days yet to come.

I come softly into the still white home of pain, and lips that are too weak to speak just tremble in silent, eloquent gratitude.

In a thousand ways I cause the weary world to look up into the face of God, and for a little moment forget the things that are small and wretched.

I am the Christmas Spirit!

E. C. BAIRD

✥✥✥

GLORIA IN EXCELSIS

The highest is ever in the lowest found:
For kings are clad in common cloths,
And love is to a stable bound,
And Christ upon a cross—
Is crowned!

DONALD J. CUNNINGHAM

✥✥✥

GOD WITH MAN

From the day of the Nativity God was with man, not simply as heretofore, as the Omnipresent, but under new and more intimate conditions.

From the day of the Nativity there was a change in the relations between earth and heaven.

To be one with Christ was to be one with God; and this union with God through Christ is the secret and basis of the new kingdom of souls which Christ has founded, and in which He reigns.

Who shall describe the wealth of spiritual and moral power which dates from the appearance of the Incarnate Son in our human world, as our "Wisdom, and Righteousness, and Sanctification, and Redemption"?

Here and there we see through the clouds, as though by glimpses, some streaks of the glory of this Invisible Kingdom of souls; but only in another life shall we understand at all approximately what it has meant for millions of our race.

H. P. LIDDON

❖❖❖

It is not even the beginning of Christmas unless it is Christmas in the heart.

RICHARD ROBERTS

❖❖❖

THE HUMILITY OF MARY

What was it that the Bethlehem innkeeper really shut out when he closed the door in the face of Mary, the mother of Jesus?

What were the qualities of heart that Mary embodied and carried with her to the stable, as over against the qualities embodied by some blustering bejeweled merchant from Capernaum whom the innkeeper eagerly admitted?

One of these qualities was humility. Mary knew in her heart that her child was destined to unexampled greatness. But this did not seem to her to be a reason for demanding a place in the inn.

She preferred that her Baby should be born in a manger surrounded only by those who loved Him.

WENDELL P. KEELER

❖❖❖

DOMINANT FIGURE

We date all events on earth from the time of the coming of Jesus and "His is easily the dominant figure of history."

That is astounding—especially to anyone who has been in the country where He lived, has visited the little village where He grew up, has sensed the poverty of it all, the slim chance He had, the few years He lived, the bitter enemies He made, the unpromising followers He gathered.

It is astonishing that He should be the dominant figure in history. He knew nothing about our modern science. He never invented anything. He never wrote a book. He had no wealth, no prestige, little formal education.

When still a young man, He died on Calvary; and who then could have guessed that history would even mention Him in her footnotes?

Yet He has become the dominant figure in history! Whatever other explanations may be given, this central fact should not be forgotten: here at least was one son of man to whom the Divine was vividly real.

He did not simply believe in God or have opinions about God. Multitudes of people do that. God to Him was a genuine, vitally experienced Fact, and His beatitude is autobiography: "Blessed are the pure in heart; for they shall see God."

HARRY EMERSON FOSDICK

❖❖❖

MARY, WHEN THAT LITTLE CHILD

Mary, when that little child
   Lay upon your heart at rest,
Did the thorns, Maid-mother mild,
   Pierce your breast?

Mary, when that little child
   Softly kissed your cheek benign,
Did you know, O Mary mild,
   Judas' sign?

Mary, when that little child
   Cooed and prattled at your knee,
Did you see with heart-beat wild,
   Calvary?

ROSE TRUMBULL

❖❖❖

INSIDE OF CHRISTMAS

The outside of Christmas is visible. You can see it. It is there in Christmas trees, in holly, in gay store windows, in gifts wrapped in bright paper. The outside of Christmas can be heard, in chimes, in carols, in organ music, in the voices of the choir, in sleighbells. The outside of Christmas can be tasted, in the turkey and cranberry sauce, the pumpkin pie and the candy.

In the hurry and scurry of the Christmas season most of us are so busy that we do not have time to get inside Christmas, so Christmas becomes for us a surface experience.

To discover the true riches of the Christmas season we must penetrate beneath the surface. And when we get inside of Christmas, Christmas will get inside of us.

Each of us must go adventuring to find the inside of Christmas in his own way.

We must get away from the turmoil and outward excitement that are so much a part of the outside of Christmas.

We must seek the inside of Christmas in the silence; we must look for it in our deeper selves.

We may find it alone in a cathedral, or sitting before the fire in our homes after all the others have retired.

We may take a long walk under the stars, or through the softly falling snow.

We may sit by the bedside of a sleeping little one and think about the miracle of childhood.

When we take the time to seek and find the inside of Christmas, the Christmas spirit will glow with a new radiance within our hearts.

THE RIGHT HAND

❖❖❖

HOUSEWIFE

Mary toiled in Nazareth
   Sweeping, spinning, weaving, too,
Till the oleanders' breath
   Trembled in the twilight dew,
And then, turning from the loom,
   When the humble board was spread
While the candle mocked the gloom,
   Listened for her loved ones' tread.

Mary met them at the door,
   Joseph and their slender Son,
Smiled and kissed their lips once more,
   And, their calloused fingers done
With the labors of the day,
   All their faces free from care,
Laughing ghosts of grief away,
   Bowed and blessed their simple fare.

Mary heard the olive trees
   Whisper as she sat and sewed
With Christ's head upon her knees,
   While the candle softly glowed
Over Joseph in his chair,
   Nodding, and she sighed and said
With her worn hands on his hair,
   "Lad, the stars call us to bed!"

EDGAR DANIEL KRAMER

Jordan River

. . . commit thy way unto the Lord

COMMITMENT

✦✦✦

SCRIPTURE

Commit thy way unto the Lord; trust also in him; and he shall bring it to pass. And he shall bring forth thy righteousness as the light, and thy judgment as the noonday.

PSALM 37:5-6

Then cometh Jesus from Galilee to Jordan unto John, to be baptized of him. But John forbad him, saying, I have need to be baptized of thee, and comest thou to me? And Jesus answering said unto him, Suffer it to be so now: for thus it becometh us to fulfil all righteousness. Then he suffered him. And Jesus, when he was baptized, went up straightway out of the water: and, lo, the heavens were opened unto him, and he saw the Spirit of God descending like a dove, and lighting upon him: and lo a voice from heaven, saying, This is my beloved Son, in whom I am well pleased.

MATTHEW 3:13-17

Jesus answered, Verily, verily, I say unto thee, Except a man be born of water and of the Spirit, he cannot enter into the kingdom of God. That which is born of the flesh is flesh; and that which is born of the Spirit is spirit. Marvel not that I said unto thee, Ye must be born again.

JOHN 3:5-7

✦✦✦

MEDITATION

Down to the sacred wave
The Lord of life was led;
And He who came our souls to save
In Jordan bowed His head.

John the Baptist came from the wilderness of Judea, exclaiming, "Repent ye: for the kingdom of heaven is at hand," and urging "the baptism of repentance for the remission of sins."

Jesus sought John that He might be baptized, not for Himself as a confession of sin, but "to fulfill all righteousness." This means that Jesus considered His baptism to be a rite whereby His conse-cration of Himself to God might be made manifest.

John hesitated, saying, "I indeed baptize . . . with water; but one mightier than I cometh . . . he shall baptize you with the Holy Ghost and with fire."

Whether by water or the Spirit, baptism in Christ's name, which follows confession of sin and commitment to Christ, provides entrance into the Church Universal.

Tradition says that Jesus was baptized near the place where Elisha told the Syrian commander Naaman to wash himself seven times and not far from the "exceeding high mountain" where Christ was tempted.

91

SYMBOLIC ACT

Jesus' public ministry began, His vocation as Redeemer was initiated, by a symbolic act. He was baptized in the Jordan River by a God-appointed man, a rugged ascetic called John.

"The Word became flesh." God's eternal Son identified Himself in baptism with the whole human family, which stood in need of forgiveness and spiritual rebirth.

The significance for God, men, and history of Christ's acceptance of His vocation is enshrined in the words that sounded from on high, "Thou art my beloved Son: with thee I am well pleased."

Upon the head of the newly baptized Stranger a dove descended. The dove symbolized the Holy Spirit.

God had sent the Spirit as the seal of His abiding presence with the Galilean in His redemptive mission and to supply the power needed for its accomplishment.

JOHN A. MACKAY

CHRISTLIKENESS

To become like Christ is the only thing in the world worth caring for, the thing before which every ambition of man is folly and all lower achievement vain.

HENRY DRUMMOND

BEACON LIGHT

Whenever I come on kelp-stained nets
    Drying along the sands,
I think of four bronzed fishermen,
    And my heart understands
How joyfully they laid aside
    Their nets by Galilee
To follow one clear Beacon Light
    Across eternity.

LESLIE SAVAGE CLARK

From THE BREWING OF SOMA

In simple trust like theirs who heard,
    Beside the Syrian sea,
The gracious calling of the Lord,
Let us, like them, without a word,
    Rise up and follow Thee.

JOHN GREENLEAF WHITTIER

When the Holy Spirit specially touches and stirs the heart, then prayer is wont to become very hot.

MARTIN LUTHER

THE WILDERNESS

Up from the Jordan straight His way He took
    To that lone wilderness, where rocks are hurled,
And strewn, and piled—as if the ancient world
    In strong convulsions seethed and writhed and shook,
Which heaved the valleys up, and sunk each brook,
    And flung the molten rock like ribbons curled
In midst of gray around the mountains whirled:—
    A grim land, of a fierce, forbidding look.
The wild beasts haunt its barren stony heights,
    And wilder visions came to tempt Him there;
For forty days and forty weary nights,
    Alone He faced His mortal self and sin,
Chaos without, and chaos reigned within,
    Subdued and conquered by the might of prayer.

CAROLINE HAZARD

"SPEAK, LORD, FOR THY SERVANT HEARETH"

Hush'd was the evening hymn,
 The temple courts were dark;
The lamp was burning dim
 Before the sacred ark:
When suddenly a voice Divine
 Rang through the silence of the shrine.

The old man, meek and mild,
 The priest of Israel slept;
His watch, the temple child,
 The little Levite kept.
And what from Eli's sense was seal'd
 The Lord to Hannah's son reveal'd.

Oh! give me Samuel's ear,
 The open ear, O Lord,
Alive and quick to hear
 Each whisper of Thy word;
Like him to answer at Thy call
 And to obey Thee first of all.

Oh! give me Samuel's heart,
 A lively heart that waits,
Where in Thy house Thou art,
 Or watches at Thy gates.
By day and night, a heart that still
 Moves at the breathing of Thy will.

Oh! give me Samuel's mind,
 A sweet unmurmuring faith,
Obedient and resign'd,
 To Thee in life and death,
That I may read with childlike eyes,
 Truths that are hidden from the wise.

JAMES DRUMMOND BORTHWICK

❖❖❖

The world needs the simple gospel preached and lived by men and women who believe it with all their minds and love it with all their hearts.

ROY H. SHORT

❖❖❖

THE ASCENDING WAY

It is uphill all the way from Jericho to Jerusalem; a weary road for sandaled feet— with a Cross at the top. That was the seen ascent. The unseen ascent was in the clear vision of consequence and the complete consecration to His Father's will with which Jesus went to His passion.

The great ways of life are always ascending ways. Duty is an ascent from aimless irresponsibility; knowledge an ascent from ignorance; goodness an ascent from evil deeds and imaginations; love an ascent from self and selfishness. Faith is an ascent from the seen to the unseen. The spiritual is always on the higher-up side of life.

GAIUS GLENN ATKINS

❖❖❖

DEDICATION

Holy Jesus, Thou art born
 For my sake on Christmas morn.
Lord, as Thou art born for me,
 I am born again to Thee.

Through the city and abroad,
 Thou dost lead me unto God.
Wheresoe'er Thou leadest me,
 Master, I will follow Thee.

To Thy love my love I give,
 Thou dost die that I may live.
As Thou giv'st Thy life for me,
 Lord, I give my life to Thee.

From the tomb I see Thee rise,
 When the morning fills the skies.
Lord, as Thou art risen for me,
 I will rise from death to Thee.

VICTORIA SAFFELLE JOHNSON

❖❖❖

TWO HANDS

God has given us two hands: one to receive with and the other to give with.

BILLY GRAHAM

RESOLUTION

I will, like Paul, forget those things which are behind and press forward;

like David, lift up mine eyes unto the hills from whence cometh my help;

like Abraham, trust implicitly in my God;

like Enoch, walk in daily fellowship with my heavenly Father;

like Jehosaphat, prepare my heart to seek God;

like Moses, choose rather to suffer than to enjoy the pleasures of sin for a season;

like Daniel, commune with God at all times;

like Job, be patient under all circumstances;

like Caleb and Joshua, refuse to be discouraged because of superior numbers;

like Joseph, turn my back on all evil advances;

like Gideon, advance even though my friends be few;

like Aaron and Hur, uphold the hands of my pastor and the leaders of my church with my prayer and support;

like Andrew, strive to lead my brother to Christ;

like Stephen, manifest a forgiving spirit toward all who seek my hurt.

Realizing that I cannot hope to achieve these objectives by my own strength, I will rely upon Christ, knowing that "I can do all things through Christ who strengtheneth me."

GEORGE BURGER

SIGHT

In Nazareth He knew each narrow street,
  The twisted paths that up the hillside crept,
The gleam of Galilee, where many a fleet
  Of white-sailed vessels moved. He knew where swept
The terror of the ruthless Roman swords;
  And, as he deftly planed his shining boards,
Of men, like books, he read the souls of them;
  Yet, "set his Face toward Jerusalem."

Past the long, tortured road his Spirit saw,
  Further than broken lives, than ancient law,
Beyond the scourge, the cross, the bitter death,
  His vision cast its flaming, living breath.

Two thousand years! And still we grope for light!
  Have mercy on us, Lord, and give us sight.

IDA NORTON MUNSON

HOW GOD COMES

It is a primary truth of Christianity that God reaches man directly. No person is insulated. As ocean floods the inlets, as sunlight environs the plant, so God enfolds and enwreathes the finite spirit. There is this difference, however, inlet and plant are penetrated whether they will or not. Sea and sunshine crowd themselves in a tergo. Not so with God. He can be received only through appreciation and conscious appropriation. He comes only through doors that are purposely opened for Him. A man may live as near God as the bubble is to the ocean and yet not find Him.

RUFUS M. JONES

✥✥✥

NAZARETH

What rendered You
    Immune to strife?
Was it those years
    Of country life:

Was it those times
    You climbed the hill
That trained You for
    The Father's will?

Was it while there
    You planed the wood
You learned the art
    Of doing good?

Did men condemn
    Your yokes and 'shares
And blame You when
    The fault was theirs?

What strengthened You
    To die your Death?
Was it those years
    At Nazareth?

Remind us, Lord,
    Who blench and brood,
Of Your divine
    Apprenticehood.

JOHNSTONE G. PATRICK

✥✥✥

WHO IS GOD?

God is to you and me, to our deepest thought concerning Him, life of our life, soul of our souls.

God is the object of our aspirations, the source of our inspirations, revealer of something of His sacred will in our consciences, comfort in our distresses, power in our weakness, wisdom in our ignorance, guide in our darkness, forgiver of our sins.

God it is who purifies and uplifts and ennobles our souls.

God it is who gives us the sense that we are not alone in the world and that we shall not be put to confusion.

God it is who gives us the sense of victory, not perhaps in this world, certainly not wholly in this world, but victory over the world, even when all things in the world have gone against us.

God it is through whom we feel that nothing in heaven or earth is of consequence if only we have hold on Him and He has hold on us.

God it is who is revealed in the love and faithfulness of men and women, in the purity of little children, in the grand strife of men on behalf of an ideal in life, in the joy of sacrifice which brave souls have had, in the heroism of death, and in the confidence of immortal life.

God it is whom we feel to have dwelt among us full of grace and truth in the spirit of Jesus.

God it is who, in dwelling in transcendent measure in Jesus, has revealed to us in greater measure what life means, what man is for, and how we have to think of the just and loving, the holy and compassionate, the invisible and ineffable God Himself.

EDWARD CALDWELL MOORE

✥✥✥

Give me twelve men who are wholly surrendered to God, and I will convert the world with them. To give and not to count the cost; to fight and not to heed the wounds; to strive and not to seek for rest; to labor and to ask for no reward, saving the knowledge that we do God's will.

IGNATIUS OF LOYOLA

✥✥✥

FORGETFUL OF SELF

To give heart and mind to God, so that they are ours no longer; to do good without being conscious of it; to pray cease-lessly and without effort, as we breathe; to love without stopping to reflect upon our feelings; to go ever onward without paus-ing to measure our progress—such is the perfect forgetfulness of self which casts us upon God, as a babe rests upon its mother's breast. It is not by great deeds, long prayers, or even by heavy crosses that we may best give glory to God; self-will may taint all these, but total self-renunciation does in truth give Him all the glory.

J. N. GROU

HOLINESS

Holiness means belonging to God and being like God. It involves doing what is right. But most of all it involves acting as the instrument of His saving work.

NORMAN SNAITH

JUDAH'S HALLOWED BARDS

Let those who will hang rapturously o'er
  The flowing eloquence of Plato's page;
Repeat, with flashing eyes, the sounds that pour
  From Homer's verse as with a torrent's rage;
Let those who list ask Sully to assuage
  Wild hearts with high-wrought periods, and restore
The reign of rhetoric; or maxims sage
  Winnow from Seneca's sententious lore.
Not these, but Judah's hallowed bards, to me
Are dear: Isaiah's noble energy;
The temperate grief of Job; the artless strain
  Of Ruth and pastoral Amos; the high songs
  Of David; and the tale of Joseph's wrongs,
Simple, pathetic, eloquently plain.

AUBREY THOMAS DE VERE

Whoever sets out to follow Christ will have to follow Him a long way, and to follow Him into some dark places. Easy enough while the road runs by the shining shores of the Lake of Galilee, but not so easy when it turns into the Garden of Gethsemane and becomes the Via Dolo-rosa.

L. P. JACKS

Loyalty to Christ is the highest loyalty known to mankind and only those who are loyal to Him have a right to bear His name and be known as His followers. "Lovest thou me?" was the first and last question of Christ to His apostles, and it is His first and last question to men today.

JOHN MC DOWELL

BARTIMEUS

God, grant to us Thy blessed Gift again,
  To walk with us, as once in Galilee—
Talking of pebbles, and of birds o'erhead;
  Of little children, and our daily bread—
To us, Thy lowly fisher-folk! Make plain
  The shining wonder of Himself again
That we may touch the seamless garment's hem,
  And be made whole of selfishness and sin;
Behold, the hearts made humble and con-trite—
  Lord, that we may at last receive our sight!

LAURA SIMMONS

I have loved to hear my Lord spoken of, and wherever I have seen the print of His shoe in the earth, there have I coveted to put mine also.

JOHN BUNYAN

❖❖❖

FOLLOW ME

And Him evermore I beheld
   Walking in Galilee;
Through the cornfield's waving gold,
   In hamlet, in wood, in wold,
By the shores of the Beautiful Sea.
   He toucheth the sightless eyes;
Before Him the demons flee;
   To the dead He saith, "Arise!"
To the living, "Follow me!"
   And that voice shall still sound on
From the centuries that are gone
   To the centuries that shall be.

HENRY WADSWORTH LONGFELLOW

❖❖❖

PRAYER

O Thou in whom we live and move and
   have our being,
   Who hast compassed us about
With a great cloud of witnesses,
   The true-hearted and the brave,
The wise and the saintly,
   More worthily of such high company
     we would live;
May we run with patience
   The course that is set before us,
Faithful to our highest purposes,
   And sure of Thy sustaining strength.

ROBERT FRENCH LEAVENS

❖❖❖

PERSONAL INFLUENCE

It is a commonplace, confirmed by all experience, that the chief factor in moral achievement is personal influence. It works by way of word and example, and it is for this reason that we insist on the value of reading the exploits and the life-story of good men and women. But it works most powerfully through personal contact. The presence of a good man or woman with the gift of a sympathetic personality is admittedly the greatest human force in developing character.

C. W. EMMET

❖❖❖

RELATIONSHIP

No man can bring another man closer to Christ than he is himself.

DWIGHT L. MOODY

❖❖❖

FOLLOWING CHRIST

Does Christ save you from your sin?
   Call Him Savior!

Does He free you from the slavery of your
   passions?
   Call Him Redeemer!

Does He teach you as no one else has
   taught you?
   Call Him Teacher!

Does He mould and master your life?
   Call Him Master!

Does He shine upon the pathway that is
   dark to you?
   Call Him Guide!

Does He reveal God to you?
   Call Him the Son of God!

Does He reveal man?
   Call Him the Son of Man!

Or, in following Him, are your lips silent
   in your incapacity to define Him, and
   His influence upon you?
   Call Him by no name, but follow Him!

HOWARD S. BLISS

Nain

. . . He healeth the broken in heart

HEALING

SCRIPTURE

Praise ye the Lord: for it is good to sing praises unto our God. . . .
He healeth the broken in heart, and bindeth up their wounds. . . .
Great is our Lord, and of great power.

PSALM 147:1, 3, 5

Jesus answering said unto them, Go your way, and tell John what
things ye have seen and heard; how that the blind see, the lame walk,
the lepers are cleansed, the deaf hear, the dead are raised, to the poor
the gospel is preached.

LUKE 7:22

He went into a city called Nain; and many of his disciples went with
him, and much people. Now when he came nigh to the gate of the
city, behold, there was a dead man carried out, the only son of his
mother, and she was a widow: and much people of the city was with
her. And when the Lord saw her, he had compassion on her, and said
unto her, Weep not. And he came and touched the bier: and they
that bare him stood still. And he said, Young man, I say unto thee,
Arise. And he that was dead sat up, and began to speak. And he
delivered him to his mother.

LUKE 7:11–15

And the leaves of the tree were for the healing of the nations.

REVELATION 22:2

❖❖❖

MEDITATION

At the gate of the small Galilean village of Nain, six miles southeast of Nazareth, Jesus, His disciples, and "much people" paused as the body of a widow's only son was borne to a place of burial.

Few incidents in the Gospels so vividly and poignantly picture the great heart of the Lord, for when Jesus saw the mother's grief, He "had compassion on her." He spoke only three words. To the mother He said, "Weep not." Then, touching the bier, to the son He said, "Arise."

And at that hour the living relationship of that unnamed mother and her only son was joyously restored.

Gospel miracles are variously interpreted as evidences of the divine authority and power resident in Jesus and as signs of His messianic role, but the miracle of Nain tells of that most precious characteristic of Christ: His empathy and moving compassion for anyone whose need is great.

The quickening of belief, stirring of conscience, answered prayer, and Christ's residence in the heart by faith are evidences that miracles of grace sustain our daily lives.

101

THE TOUCH OF HUMAN HANDS

The touch of human hands—
  That is the boon we ask;
For groping, day by day,
  Along the stony way,
We need the comrade heart
  That understands,
And the warmth, the living warmth
  Of human hands.

The touch of human hands;
  Not vain, unthinking words,
Nor that cold charity
  Which shuns our misery;
We seek a loyal friend
  Who understands,
And the warmth, the pulsing warmth
  Of human hands.

The touch of human hands—
  Such care as was in Him
Who walked in Galilee
  Beside the silver sea;
We need a patient guide
  Who understands,
And the warmth, the loving warmth
  Of human hands.

THOMAS CURTIS CLARK

❖❖❖

When Jesus Christ met a Samaritan, met a few children, an adulterous woman, then did humanity rise three times to the level of God.

MAURICE MAETERLINCK

❖❖❖

From OUR MASTER

The healing of His seamless dress
  Is by our beds of pain;
We touch Him in life's throng and press,
  And we are whole again.

JOHN GREENLEAF WHITTIER

MAN OF THE PEOPLE

Jesus was the man of the people, who knew their joys and sorrows because He lived as one of them.

He learned life at the carpenter's bench in Nazareth.

He took our common life and daily toil and made them into divine things.

The crowded cities of Galilee were His home.

His heart went out to the helpless and the diseased, to the oppressed poor, to the rich, starved of true fellowship, and to the self-righteous, separated by their hardness of heart from their fellows and from God.

He gave Himself to men without reserve, in loving fellowship; their life and lot came into His life; those who opened their hearts to Him knew His life; and overcoming love came into their lives.

When His people refused Him and crucified Him, His love still sought them undespairing.

BOOK OF DISCIPLINE

❖❖❖

THE HEALER

He laid His hands on withered bones.
  Responsive to His touch they woke
To whisper tales. The very stones
  Beneath His friendly feet once spoke
Mysterious answers, and the dusks
  Of decades sounded in deaf ears.
Vital once more, the wasted husks
  Grew green when watered with His tears.

JOHNSTONE G. PATRICK

❖❖❖

All loving is a thanksgiving for the fact that we ourselves have been loved and healed in loving.

HELMUT THIELICKE

IN GALILEE

Erect in youthful grace and radiant
  With spirit forces, all imparadised
In a divine compassion, down the slant
  Of these remembering hills He came, the
    Christ.

Should not the glowing lilies of the field
  With keener splendor mark His foot-
    prints yet?
Prints of the gentle feet whose passing
  healed
  All blight from Tabor unto Olivet?

KATHARINE LEE BATES

✧✧✧

You cannot find a true Christian on the
face of the earth who will not tell you
that what he gave up for Christ was nothing
compared to what he received.

CHARLES TORREY

✧✧✧

THE TEN LEPERS

Not white and shining like an ardent flame,
  Not like Thy mother and the saints in
    bliss,
But white from head to foot I bear my
  blame,
  White as the leper is.

Unclean! unclean! But Thou canst make
  me clean:
  Yet if Thou clean'st me, Lord, see that
    I be
Like that one grateful leper of the ten
  Who ran back praising Thee.

But if I must forget, take back Thy word;
  Be I unclean again but not ingrate.
Before I shall forget Thee, keep me, Lord,
  A sick man at Thy gate.

KATHARINE TYNAN

THE HEM OF HIS GARMENT

O God of Calvary and Bethlehem,
  Thou who did'st suffer rather than con-
    demn,
Grant me to touch Thy garment's healing
  hem!

Thou trailest Thy fair robes of seamless
  light
  Through this dark world of misery and
    night;
Its blackness cannot mar Thy spotless white.

Thou dost not, Master, as we pass Thee by,
  Draw in Thy robes lest we should come
    too nigh;
We see no scorn in Thine all-sinless eye.

There is no shrinking even from our touch;
  Thy tenderness to us is ever such,
It can endure and suffer much.

ANNA ELIZABETH HAMILTON

✧✧✧

GOD OUR FRIEND

In this vast universe
  There is but one supreme truth—
That God is our friend!
  By that truth meaning is given
To the remote stars, the numberless cen-
  turies,
  The long and heroic struggle of man-
    kind . . .
O my Soul, dare to trust this truth!
  Dare to rest in God's kindly arms,
Dare to look confidently into His face,
  Then launch thyself into life unafraid!
Knowing thou art within thy Father's
  house,
  That thou art surrounded by His love,
Thou wilt become master of fear,
  Lord of life, conqueror even of death!

JOSHUA LOTH LIEBMAN

✧✧✧

Candlelighting is Jesus' chief business.

HAROLD W. RUOPP

❖❖❖

THE CARPENTER OF NAZARETH

In Nazareth, the narrow road,
  That tires the feet and steals the breath,
Passes the place where once abode
  The Carpenter of Nazareth.

And up and down the dusty way
  The village folk would often wend;
And on the bench, beside Him, lay
  Their broken things for Him to mend.

The maiden with the doll she broke,
  The woman with the broken chair,
The man with broken plough, or yoke,
  Said, "Can you mend it, Carpenter?"

And each received the thing he sought,
  In yoke, or plough, or chair, or doll;
The broken thing which each had brought
  Returned again a perfect whole.

So, up the hill the long years through,
  With heavy step and wistful eye,
The burdened souls their way pursue,
  Uttering each the plaintive cry:

"O Carpenter of Nazareth,
  This heart, that's broken past repair,
This life, that's shattered nigh to death,
  Oh, can You mend them, Carpenter?"

And by His kind and ready hand,
  His own sweet life is woven through
Our broken lives, until they stand
  A New Creation—"all things new."

"The shattered idols of my heart,
  Desire, ambition, hope and faith,
Mould Thou into the perfect part,
  O Carpenter of Nazareth!"

GEORGE BLAIR

❖❖❖

COUNTRY WELL CURB

Always holiness shall cling
  Around a well
Whose water mirrors dawn and star
  In depths that tell
Of Him who paused beside a curb
  To promise men
The living water all may draw—
  Nor thirst again.

LESLIE SAVAGE CLARK

❖❖❖

THE LAMP OF LOVE

There is no task so great, no road so long
  That is not brightened when
The lamp of love glows clear and strong,
  When willing hands and feet
Are grateful for its presence there,
  And hearts keep it alight with faith and
    prayer.

Love's lamp is ours to share. Help us grow
    wise,
  Holding it high that men
May see, and hope shine in their eyes;
  And brother with brother
Honor, across the earth's great lands,
  The One who lighteth it with nail-
    pierced hands.

MARY ALDRICH BEECHNER

❖❖❖

A PRAYER

I pray not for the joy that knows
  No saving benison of tears;
The placid life of ease that flows
  Untroubled through the changing years.

Grant me, O God, the mind to see
  The blessings which my sorrows bring;
And give me, in adversity,
  The heart that still can trust and sing.

MARION FRANKLIN HAM

❖❖❖

THE WOMAN WHO CAME BEHIND
HIM IN THE CROWD

Near Him she stole, rank after rank;
   She feared approach too loud;
She touched His garment's hem, and shrank,
   Back in the sheltering crowd.

A shame-faced gladness thrills her frame:
   Her twelve years' fainting prayer
Is heard at last! she is the same
   As other women there!

She hears His voice. He looks about,
   Ah! is it kind or good
To drag her secret sorrow out
   Before that multitude?

The eyes of men she dares not meet—
   On her they straight must fall!
Forward she sped, and at His feet
   Fell down, and told Him all.

To the one refuge she hath flown,
   The Godhead's burning flame!
Of all earth's women she alone
   Hears there the tenderest name!

"Daughter," He said, "be of good cheer;
   Thy faith hath made thee whole";
With plenteous love, not healing mere,
   He comforteth her soul.

GEORGE MACDONALD

A PRAYER

O Lord, the hard-won miles
   Have worn my stumbling feet:
Oh, soothe me with Thy smiles,
   And make my life complete.

The thorns were thick and keen
   Where'er I trembling trod;
The way was long between
   My wounded feet and God.

Where healing waters flow
   Do Thou my footsteps lead.
My heart is aching so;
   Thy gracious balm I need.

PAUL LAURENCE DUNBAR

BIRTHDAY MESSAGE
FOR A DEAR FRIEND

Because I love you I would send
You lovely things that never end:
Contentment like a high white star,
A pansy's purple calendar,
The sound of little creatures' feet
Along a tiny grass-green street,
The quietness of dusk-blue air,
The healing sanctity of prayer,
And faith, a wonder-lighted chart
For constellations of the heart.

GRACE V. WATKINS

THE HANDS OF CHRIST

A Baby's hands in Bethlehem
   Were small and softly curled,
But held within their dimpled grasp
   The hope of half the world.

A Carpenter's in Nazareth
   Were skilled with tool and wood;
They laid the beams of simple homes
   And found their labor good.

A Healer's hands in Galilee
   Were stretched to all who came
For Him to cleanse their hidden wounds
   Or cure the blind and lame.

Long, long ago the hands of Christ
   Were nailed upon a tree,
But still their holy touch redeems
   The hearts of you and me.

LESLIE SAVAGE CLARK

Dead Sea

. . . for judgment I am come into this world

JUDGMENT

✤✤✤

SCRIPTURE

Blessed is the man that walketh not in the counsel of the ungodly, nor standeth in the way of sinners, nor sitteth in the seat of the scornful. But his delight is in the law of the Lord; and in his law doth he meditate day and night. And he shall be like a tree planted by the rivers of water, that bringeth forth his fruit in his season; his leaf also shall not wither; and whatsoever he doeth shall prosper.

PSALM 1:1–3

Watch ye therefore, and pray always, that ye may be accounted worthy . . . to stand before the Son of man.

LUKE 21:36

As I live, saith the Lord, every knee shall bow to me, and every tongue shall confess to God. So then every one of us shall give account of himself to God.

ROMANS 14:11–12

Behold, I stand at the door, and knock: if any man hear my voice, and open the door, I will come in to him, and will sup with him, and he with me.

REVELATION 3:20

✤✤✤

MEDITATION

"I will sing of mercy and judgment," wrote the psalmist. The loving-kindness of God counterbalances the obedience He requires of His children. Inescapable obligation is laid upon us, and responsibility to self, man, and God is incumbent in the Christian's calling. Knowingly Paul wrote, "We shall all stand before the judgment seat of Christ."

Nothing in the Holy Land more suggestively symbolizes judgment than does the Dead Sea, under whose waters, according to ancient tradition, lie the doomed cities "of the plain," Sodom and Gomorrah.

The Dead Sea, which receives the fresh waters of the Jordan River, has no outlet and therefore its saltiness is five times greater than that of the ocean. It is incapable of nourishing and sustaining life. The brackish waters, framed by high, barren cliffs, are reminiscent of descriptions found in Dante's *Inferno*.

Our lives, like Lot's wife who was turned into a pillar of salt because she disobeyed the divine word, are judged worthless when we reject the heavenly vision.

"Where is the Life that we have lost in living?" is T. S. Eliot's haunting question, but our hope in Christ is found in His words, "I came not to judge the world, but to save it."

CONDEMNATION

We speak of Light descending as a dove
Upon the tortured ignorance of those
Who knew this condemnation—that they
    chose
The way of darkness, being warned thereof.
Surely the Light that shone then, wide
    above
Those lifted hands, shines now, and still
    bestows
Its promised freedom to the heart that
    knows
The bright day and the open way of love.

"But men chose darkness," thus the Scrip-
    tures run,
"Because their deeds were evil." Is this
    night
Of our own choosing? Do we fear the Light?
What are the evil things that we have done,
That we must tap a stick upon a stone,
And move like blind men, fearful and
    alone?

SARA KING CARLETON

❖❖❖

VERBS

I *am:* the power of self-knowledge.
I *think:* the power to investigate.
I *know:* the power to master facts.
I *feel:* the power to appreciate, to value,
    and to love.
I *wonder:* the power of reverence, curiosity,
    and worship.
I *see:* the power of insight, imagination, and
    vision.
I *believe:* the power of adventurous faith.
I *can:* the power to act and the skill to
    accomplish.
I *ought:* the power of conscience and the
    moral imperative.
I *serve:* the power to be useful and devoted
    to a cause.

GEORGE WALTER FISKE

❖❖❖

DIES IRAE

There were no footprints left upon the
    waters
    When Jesus walked on Lake Gennesaret.
The unrecorded words His finger penciled
    In dust upon the road are gone like
    breath.
Yet when the charts and books are all dis-
    carded,
    And, dreadful is the dawn, the horn is
    heard
Above the ended roads, the canceled
    phrases,
    Behold! the endless Way, the deathless
    Word!

JAMES L. DUFF

❖❖❖

When all light is God's light, when all
love is God's love, when all things are God's
things—then surprise is the interior climate
of life.

JOSEPH SITTLER

❖❖❖

PRAYER

Thou, who didst once wander on earth,
leaving footprints which we should follow;

Thou, who still from Thy heaven dost
look down upon each wanderer, dost
strengthen the weary, encourage the de-
spondent, comfort the striving;

Thou who also at the end of days shalt
return to judge whether each man individu-
ally has followed Thee:

Our God and our Savior, let Thine
example stand clearly before the eyes of our
soul to disperse the mists;

Strengthen us that unfalteringly we may
keep this before our eyes; that we by resem-
bling and following Thee may later find the
way to the judgment, for it behooves every
man to be brought to the judgment, oh, but
also through Thee to be brought to eternal
happiness hereafter with Thee.

SØREN KIERKEGAARD

❋❋❋

Along the selfsame road we came
    Simon Peter and I;
The shame of fearful words he fled;
    I, of a living lie.

A lonely way of pain it was
    For Simon Peter then;
To him there came the end, but I
    Must walk it oft again.

                    EARL EDWARD YOST

❋❋❋

"IF ANY MAN WOULD"

May not I drop the cross that grows so
        heavy,
    Shorten the furrow-length that seems so
        long;
Must I pay tribute that the lilies levy,
    Thrill to no music but a sparrow's song?

"Yea," speaks a voice all-gentle and all-
        knowing,
    "Lighten your cross, look backward from
        your plow;
Gather the beauty your own hand is sowing,
    Dance to the tune your heart is singing
        now.

"Choose! But recall in fortune or disaster—
    Since 'tis yourself alone in judgment
        sits—
Who bears no cross follows another master
    Who backward looks, another kingdom
        fits."

                EDWIN MC NEILL POTEAT

❋❋❋

SERVANT

Paul is the Christian Hercules, and his labors are so varied and wonderful, that we sometimes lose the man in the blaze of the glory of the things he accomplished.

It was he who lifted the Christian religion out of its Palestinian cradle, tore away its swaddling clothes, and trained it to walk along the highways of the Roman Empire.

It was he who clipped the shell, and set the imprisoned eagle free.

It was he who lit the first Christian lamp in the palace of the Caesars.

It was he who converted a Jewish sect into a world religion.

It was he who saw Jesus not simply as a Jewish Messiah, but as the divine Savior of all mankind.

It was he who placed the cross of Jesus at the center of human history, and also at the center of the universe.

It was he who broke down the wall of separation between the Jew and the Gentile, and gathered all men into one family of God.

It was he who changed the religious atmosphere of the world. That atmosphere was charged with legalism and ceremonialism, and he, like a thunderstorm, came sweeping across the world, and by the flashes of lightning from his hot soul, he changed the air forever.

He penned paragraphs so beautiful and with such healing in them, that they will be read in the public worship of Christian congregations to the last day.

His name is above every name except the name of Jesus. Like his Master he was great because he was the servant of all.

                CHARLES E. JEFFERSON

❋❋❋

I find that a life of little whispered words of adoration, of praise, of prayer, of worship can be breathed all through the day. One can have a very busy day, outwardly speaking, and yet be steadily in the holy Presence. It is a life unspeakable and full of glory, an inner world of splendor within which we, unworthy, may live.

                THOMAS R. KELLY

❋❋❋

111

WHEN JESUS WASHED THE FEET OF JUDAS

What were His thoughts,
    What grieving tore His heart,
What pity drove Him to the bitter part,
    When He, the Lord, fell on His knees
To wash the feet of Judas?

None saw a frown,
    Nay, did not he, the traitor, feel
A tender pressure on his sordid heel,
    When He, the Lord, fell on His knees
To wash the feet of Judas?

Straight from His heart
    What passion burst and pled
To call a blinded comrade from the dead,
    When He, the Lord, fell on His knees
To wash the feet of Judas?

Was there no stir
    Within the traitor's soul, no strife,
No stirrings from the dead to life,
    When He, the Lord, fell on His knees
To wash the feet of Judas?

Black was the night,
    No moonbeam fell across His dark,
A comrade's soul was dead and stark,
    After our Lord, upon His knees,
Had washed the feet of Judas.

            RALPH SPAULDING CUSHMAN

❖❖❖

THE PHARISEE

Too carefully he scrutinized
How well men kept the horde
Of petty laws, the tithe of mint,
The trivial reward.
So close he bent, he failed to see
The presence of his Lord.

            LESLIE SAVAGE CLARK

❖❖❖

BETRAYAL

Still as of old
    Men by themselves are priced—

For thirty pieces Judas sold
    Himself, not Christ.

            HESTER H. CHOLMONDELEY

❖❖❖

ONE LIGHT, ONE LOVE

The world is dark on many sides,
    Still darker is the thought within;
Satanic furies take their rides,
    And much is not what might have been.

Yet over all of this abides
    That fact with which all days begin:
One Light the threatening dark derides;
    One Love can cancel every sin.

            KENDIG BRUBAKER CULLY

❖❖❖

AMOS, THE PROPHET OF JUSTICE

For three sins, and a fourth, God's wrath
    was stirred.
    His chosen people wallowed in the dust;
They laughed at justice, served the gods of
    lust,
    Oppressed the poor, and scorned His
    Holy Word.
But there was one who reverenced the good,
    Who worshipped God and tried His will
    to do—
The herdsman Amos, simple, plain and
    true.
    Said God: "Go say their sin is under-
    stood."
So Amos: "God, the mighty Lord of earth,
    Hath known your sins and ye shall reap
    reward
For all your wrongs. A strong and cruel
    horde
    Shall devastate your land. In bitter
    dearth
Ye shall abide, and from your homes shall
    go
    To alien realms, a land of wrath and
    woe."

            THOMAS CURTIS CLARK

Life is before you—not earthly life alone, but life—a thread running interminably through the warp of eternity.

JOSIAH GILBERT HOLLAND

❖❖❖

TEMPTATION

They took Him to a mountain-top to see
　Where earth's fair kingdoms flung their
　　golden net
To snare the feet and trick the souls of men.
　With slimy craft and cynic guile they said:
If He but sees the glory and the pride,
　The pomps and pleasures of this tinsel
　　world,
He will forget His splendid, futile dreams;
　And so they took Him up and tempted
　　Him.

They pointed far across their level earth,
　East to the fabled empires of the Ind,
Whose rulers' power was as the power of
　　gods,
　Where caravans with tinkling camel-bells
Brought silks and perfumes, pearls and
　　ivory,
　And tribute from far humbled provinces;
South to the magic kingdom of the Nile,
　To Nubia and Abyssinia,
Jungle and desert kingdoms, rude but rich
　With slaves and gems and golden yellow
　　sands;
Northward to barbarous lands but dimly
　　seen,
　Savage but surging with unmeasured
　　strength;
West where Rome's empire sent her legions
　　forth,
　Conquering, building, ruling with wise
　　force,
The mighty mother of an unborn brood
　Of nations which should rise and rule the
　　world.

All this they spread before Him, tempting
　　Him,
　And watched to see ambition light His
　　eye,
The lust of power darken His bright face,

And avarice crook His hands to clutch
　the gold.

But from the mountain peak He raised His
　eyes,
　And saw the deep, calm sky, the stars, and
　God.

WINFRED ERNEST GARRISON

❖❖❖

Man is the meeting place of two worlds, and however closely his mind and labor may be tied to the visible world, he has never forgotten his lofty destiny.

NATHAN SÖDERBLOM

❖❖❖

JOSES, THE BROTHER OF JESUS

Joses, the brother of Jesus, plodded from
　day to day
　With never a vision within him to glorify
　his clay;
Joses, the brother of Jesus, was only a
　worker in wood,
　And he never could see the glory, that
　Jesus, his brother, could.
"Why stays He not in the workshop?" he
　often used to complain,
　"Sawing the Lebanon cedar, imparting to
　woods their stain?
Why must He go thus roaming, forsaking
　my father's trade,
　While hammers are busily sounding, and
　there is gain to be made?"
Thus ran the mind of Joses, apt with
　plummet and rule,
　And deeming whoever surpassed him
　either a knave or a fool.—
For he never walked with the prophets in
　God's great garden of bliss—
　And of all the mistakes of the ages, the
　saddest methinks, was this:
To have such a brother as Jesus, to speak
　with Him day by day,
　But never to catch the vision that glori-
　fied His Clay.

HARRY KEMP

Mount Sinai

. . . the voice of the Law

LAW

❖❖❖

And the Lord came down upon mount Sinai, on the top of the mount: and the Lord called Moses up to the top of the mount; and Moses went up. . . . And God spake all these words, saying. . . . Thou shalt have no other gods before me. Thou shalt not make unto thee any graven image. . . . Thou shalt not take the name of the Lord thy God in vain. . . . Remember the sabbath day, to keep it holy. . . . Honour thy father and thy mother. . . . Thou shalt not kill. Thou shalt not commit adultery. Thou shalt not steal. Thou shalt not bear false witness against thy neighbour. Thou shalt not covet.

EXODUS 19:20; 20:1, 3–17

Open thou mine eyes, that I may behold wondrous things out of thy law.

PSALM 119:18

What doth the Lord require of thee, but to do justly, and to love mercy, and to walk humbly with thy God.

MICAH 6:8

Thou shalt love the Lord thy God with all thy heart, and with all thy soul, and with all thy mind, and with all thy strength: this is the first commandment. And the second is like, namely this, Thou shalt love thy neighbour as thyself.

MARK 12:30–31

❖❖❖

MEDITATION

Three months following their deliverance from the Egyptian yoke, the Israelites encamped at the foot of Mount Sinai. On the mountain God gave Moses the Ten Commandments. The Law became the instrument whereby the Israelites might achieve ethical and moral responsibility.

Free men, then and now, are free because of their acceptance and respect for law, whether sacred or secular.

Although the Decalogue is expressed in negations, our spiritual ancestors did not consider the law to be oppressive or restrictive. Rather, the law was joyously em-braced and coveted. The writer of Psalm 119 exclaimed, "O how love I thy law! it is my meditation all the day," adding, "Thy word is a lamp unto my feet, and a light unto my path."

Christ, who cherished the law of His people, enlarged its spirit by emphasizing humanitarian principles and love.

Christ obligates us not only to "render . . . unto Caesar the things which are Caesar's," meaning obedience insofar as conscience permits to the law of man, but also to the higher and more exacting law of love exemplified by His life and words.

117

From THE HEAVENLY LIGHT

When all the world was steeped in sin,
   The Hebrews braved the nations' wrath
And nobly followed still the guide
   That led them on in virtue's path.

That beacon is the Decalogue,
   Proclaimed from Sinai's flaming height,
And burning, as each age rolls by,
   With purer, grander, holier light.

Oh, glorious flame! thy sparkling beams
   With radiant splendor shine today;
Nor time, nor change, nor tyrant's power
   Can quench or dim one holy ray.

Oh, heavenly lamp! thy light shall shine
   Till sin and hate from earth depart,
Till wrong shall fail and right prevail,
   And justice rule the human heart.

May that bright beacon guide us still,
   E'en like God's own untiring hand,
That we, when this life's storms are o'er,
   May reach with joy the heavenly land.

MAX MEYERHARDT

CELESTIAL LAWS

The best things in life, the loveliest things, are a result of obedience.

How did we get this morning's sunrise, and how shall we have this evening's sunset? Because the earth is conforming to a pattern fashioned by the Creator.

There are celestial laws that govern the turning of our earth in space. The earth is never stubbornly disobedient to these laws. The earth is obedient to the celestial laws and that obedience makes the earth habitable.

HAROLD E. KOHN

BEFORE THE TEN COMMANDMENTS

Before the Ten Commandments, came the
   Word:
   In the beginning. God unloosed the bars,
Created earth, the sun, the nesting bird,
   The cattle for a thousand hills, and stars;
He founded bread within the scroll of seed;
   The waters came and filled the wells of
   earth;
Only when He had met man's every need
   Was man raised up from the dust, and
   given birth
With all dominion over living things.
   He knew the sweet companionship of
   mate,
The touch of trusting deer, the wing that
   sings.
   Still, in the midst of such a love, lived
   hate.
How ached the heart of God when He fore-
   saw
   That man would also need the stone of
   law.

RALPH W. SEAGER

From BIBLIOLATRES

God is not dumb, that He should speak no
   more;
   If thou hast wanderings in the wilderness
And findest not Sinai, 'tis thy soul is poor;
   There towers the mountain of the Voice
   no less,
Which whoso seeks shall find; but he who
   bends,
   Intent on manna still and mortal ends,
Sees it not, neither hears its thundered lore.

Slowly the Bible of the race is writ,
   And not on paper leaves nor leaves of
   stone;
Each age, each kindred, adds a verse to it,
   Texts of despair or hope, of joy or moan.
While swings the sea, while mists the moun-
   tains shroud,

While thunder's surges burst on cliffs of
   cloud,
Still at the prophets' feet the nations sit.
JAMES RUSSELL LOWELL

❖❖❖

SOME SINAI

Each soul must seek some Sinai
   Where God's great truths are told;
Must find God's revelations
   Writ on shining plates of gold.

Some high and sacred place, apart;
   Some sky-touched mountain peak
Where he may hear the thunders roll
   And all God's voices speak.

Each soul must find some silent place;
   Some high and holy shrine
Where all the stars and suns and moons
   And plunging planets shine.

Here are God's revelations;
   Here are His thoughts, sublime
To guide all human hearts and hopes
   Through space and tide and time.

Each soul must seek some Sinai;
   Some vision-haunted place;
Some silent, sacred, singing shrine
   To see His lighted face.
WILLIAM L. STIDGER

❖❖❖

A SOUL TO WIN

Given Christ and His cross and the assurance of God's fatherhood which lives in
   them and shines through them,
given the possibilities and prophesies of
   each time-born self,
given life with its tasks, its battles, its un-
   foldings, its transforming experiences,
given this world of ours as the stage of our
   pilgrimage,
given ministrant days and loving comradeship and truth and beauty, music by

which to march, and the Dayspring from
   on high across the hills of time—
in our steadfastness we shall win our souls.
This is what life and time are for.
If this world of ours were meant for joy
   alone, its conditions are hard to justify.
If it were meant for petty success, it is not
   worth the cost.
If it were meant for smug well-being, it
   would better never have been created.
But if it be meant for a place in which to
   win a soul, then whatever worlds, teth-
   ered to other suns, are lost in far-flung
   constellations, ours is the peer of them all.
GAIUS GLENN ATKINS

❖❖❖

THE BURNING BUSH

Thy wisdom and Thy might appear,
   Eternal God, through every year;
From day to day, from hour to hour,
   Thy works reveal self-ordered power.

We worship Thee whose will hath laid
   Thy sovereign rule on all things made;
The faithful stars, the fruitful earth,
   Obey Thy laws that gave them birth.

Yet Thou canst make a marvel shine
   Amid these mighty laws of Thine,
As when Thy servant Moses came
   And saw the bush with Thee aflame.

We turn aside and tread the ways
   That lead through wonder up to praise;
Wherever Thou by man art found
   The homely earth is holy ground.

If Thou hast formed us out of dust
   Through ages long,—in Thee we trust;
O grant us in our souls to see
   The living flame that comes from Thee.
HENRY VAN DYKE

❖❖❖

THE LAW AND THE BEATITUDES

When Moses sought a mountain,
 The people shrank in dread
From billowing clouds of darkness
 Lest they be stricken dead.

When Jesus sought a mountain,
 It was a sunlit day,
And multitudes drew near Him
 And none were warned away.

When Moses left a mountain,
 The evils that he saw
Caused him to break, in anger,
 The tables of the law.

When Jesus left a mountain,
 He saw the motley, mean,
And needy crowds; and straightway
 He made a leper clean.

JANE MERCHANT

❖❖❖

COUNSEL

Man cannot break the laws of God. He can
only break himself against them.

GILBERT KEITH CHESTERTON

❖❖❖

POWER OF IDEALS

No one who is always striving to refine his
character can ever be robbed of his idealism,
for he experiences in himself the power of
the ideals of the good and true. Where there
is power, there some result or other is pro-
duced. No ray of sunlight is ever lost, but
the green which it wakes into existence
needs time to sprout, and it is not always
granted to the sower to live to see the
harvest. All work that is worth anything is
done in faith.

ALBERT SCHWEITZER

❖❖❖

THE NEW LAW

Jesus was sitting in Moses' chair.
 They brought the trembling woman
 there.
Moses commands she be stoned to death.
 What was the sound of Jesus' breath?
He laid His hand on Moses' law;
 The ancient heavens, in silent awe,
Writ with curses from pole to pole,
 All away began to roll.

WILLIAM BLAKE

❖❖❖

PROOF

When the law impels one against love, it
ceases and should no longer be a law; but
where no obstacle is in the way, the keeping
of the law is a proof of love.

MARTIN LUTHER

❖❖❖

MOSES

Like a high mountain bathed in morning
 light,
 Stands he above the tortuous centuries.
Nations have risen, grown to power and
 fame,
 Then, cursed by fate, have vanished into
 night.
But still he stands, with his stern laws God-
 lent,
 Challenging the peoples with their
 changeless truth—
Challenging the peoples, though they will
 not hear,
 Hard and stiff-necked still, proud and in-
 solent.
He still stands high above our petty men—
 Sages and judges, regnant for a day,
Pouring out laws and wisdom sacrosanct;
 Vain are the fruits of their blind brains
 and pen.
Still Moses stands, and God above His shade,
 Pitying the nations for the world they've
 made.

THOMAS CURTIS CLARK

❖❖❖

PAUL

He found life a pattern
  Woven by the Law,
And men colorless threads in the fabric,
  Save one,
Whose face shone
  As jagged stones carved the last darkness;
And Another,
  Whose light and voice
Illumined a desert road.
  Thereafter,
Frail but unafraid,
  He journeyed into the dawn—
Tearing the pattern to shreds
  To free souls
From the tyranny of the dark.

EARL MARLATT

❖❖❖

SUMAC IS A BURNING BUSH

How was it, Moses, when you saw your
  bush?
  Tell me, did spurts of red spangle the air?
Its branches crackle? Did you have to push
  Your arms before to shield your blowing
    hair?
Your eyes, did they burn in too hot to see,
  Wincing you with their scorching in your
    face?
And did you question how this shrub could
  be
  Raging a blaze, with all its leaves in place?
Now I stand here before my bush of fire,
  Braving its crimson heat upon my cheek;
Do you think, Moses, sumac could acquire
  Such brilliant flame—and no one there to
    speak?
Well, someone spoke. Though I'm not sure
  just who,
  I have the feeling, Moses, it was you.

RALPH W. SEAGER

❖❖❖

COVENANTS AND RECOMPENSE

The Law threatened
With eye-for-eye's, the negatives.
Broad Truth observed
Man gets the measure that he gives,
But Grace promised
Itself to him who too forgives.

FRANKLIN ZAHN

❖❖❖

He that strives to draw himself from obedience withdraws himself from grace.

THOMAS A KEMPIS

❖❖❖

MY BURNING BUSH FOR EVERY DAY

I have my Burning Bush each day
  As Moses had of old:
A sunrise on a mountain top,
  All crimson flame—and gold.

My Burning Bush of wild-rose bloom,
  Of phlox and goldenrod
In which I feel the presence of
  Creation and its God.

My angel of the Lord appears
  Each day when dawn is born
And I can hear the music of
  A far-off Elfland horn.

God's voice speaks to me every spring
  And I can hear His name
Where every crimson rose bush bursts
  Into a flash of flame.

WILLIAM L. STIDGER

❖❖❖

LIFE AND LOVE

He who loves not, lives not; he who lives
by the Life can never die.

RAYMOND LULL

Mount of Olives

. . . the hope that is within you

HOPE

❖❖❖

SCRIPTURE

Why art thou cast down, O my soul? and why art thou disquieted within me? hope thou in God: for I shall yet praise him, who is the health of my countenance, and my God.

PSALM 42:11

Which hope we have as an anchor of the soul, both sure and stedfast.

HEBREWS 6:19

And he led them out as far as to Bethany, and he lifted up his hands, and blessed them. And it came to pass, while he blessed them, he was parted from them, and carried up into heaven. And they worshipped him, and returned to Jerusalem with great joy.

LUKE 24:50–51

Ye men of Galilee, why stand ye gazing up into heaven? this same Jesus, which is taken up from you into heaven, shall so come in like manner as ye have seen him go into heaven.

ACTS 1:11

And I heard as it were the voice of a great multitude, and as the voice of many waters, and as the voice of mighty thunderings, saying, Alleluia: for the Lord God omnipotent reigneth.

REVELATION 19:6

❖❖❖

MEDITATION

Most noticeable of the ancient landmarks of Jerusalem is the Mount of Olives, a mile-long limestone ridge opposite the east gate and separated from the city by the valley of the Kidron.

On the Mount the disciples and a motley group of the devout and the curious assembled for the Palm Sunday procession into Jerusalem, and on the Mount, forty days after the Resurrection, they witnessed Christ's ascension.

Christian hope centers in the ascension. Christ took His place at the right hand of God the Father. He prepared, as He promised, a place for believers in His Father's house of many rooms. He became man's advocate and mediator before God, bestowed upon man the gift of the Holy Spirit, and promised that He would one day return, a hope that has strengthened and nurtured Christian faith and the Church for twenty centuries.

The Christian clarion was sounded by Paul, who wrote, "Christ in you, the hope of glory," and affirmed that it is "Jesus Christ, which is our hope."

MAN OF HOPE

No eyes ever saw more distinctly than His eyes saw the peril of human life.

He read it in every human face.

He had learned it in the temptation in the wilderness.

Only because He was God and knew the evil to be weaker than the good, He always kept the hope behind and within the danger.

Because man had in him the power to be this dreadful thing, therefore He also had in Him the power to be this splendid thing.

I know that, if we had been in Jerusalem, and had met the blessed Savior in the street, we should have read all this in His features: the fear and hope together, the hope intensified by the fear, but always conquering it and making Him eager to call every human creature with the invitation of the divine love, whose might He knew.

PHILLIPS BROOKS

MY PILOT

My bark is wafted to the strand
By breath divine,
And on the helm there rests a hand
Other than mine.

One who has known in storms to sail
I have on board;
Above the raging of the gale
I hear my Lord.

He holds me with the billows' might—
I shall not fall;
If sharp, 'tis short; if long, 'tis light;
He tempers all.

Safe to the land—safe to the land,
The end is this;
And then with him go hand in hand
Far into bliss.

WASHINGTON GLADDEN

ASCENSION LIGHT

The disciples did not know in those precious days where they could find Him, but He always knew where to find them.

It must have begun to dawn upon them that He was never really absent.

He was passing out of the Here into the Everywhere: out of the first century to fill all centuries.

It was hard for them to lose the bodily presence of Christ, the dearest thing they had ever known; but they learned. And soon they were abroad over the world offering to all men the living Christ.

A generation later Peter wrote—not without wonder—to those who had never seen Christ, "Whom having not seen ye love."

And in the generation following that, one could write, "Our fellowship is with the Father and with His Son Jesus Christ."

And this very day, East and West, North and South, there are multitudes who will say it as the deepest certainty of their lives.

"Behold I stand at the door and knock." He knocks at every door. He forces none. But there is a great company, which no man can number, who have found it true that "if any hear my voice and open the door, I will come in and sup with him and he with me."

WILLIAM RUSSELL MALBY

I seek strength,
not to be superior to my brothers,
but to be able to fight my greatest enemy—
myself.
Make me ever ready to come to You
with clean hands and straight eyes
so when life fades,
as a fading sunset,
my spirit may come to You
without shame.

SIOUX CHIEF YELLOW LARK

❖❖❖

INSPIRER OF HOPE

He is the best physician who is the most
ingenious inspirer of hope.

SAMUEL T. COLERIDGE

❖❖❖

LOT'S WIFE

I find this woman quite familiar,
Although I never learned her given name,
Or saw her smile or weep; but all the same
I find our spirits kindred. True, the far
City of Sodom and the home she lost
Are strange to me, yet I identify
With an invalidated counterpart, and try
To reconstruct her heartbreak. Was the
     cost
Of leaving friends, without farewell, in
     haste,
Too great to bear? Or was the memory of
Some small, abandoned trinket of Lot's
     love
Her cause of pain, or foodstuffs gone to
     waste?
I share her disobedience, sin, and fault.
Without God's grace, I should be turned
     to salt!

JOAN TRUITT

❖❖❖

THE GOING OF HIS FEET

His feet went here and there
     About the common earth.
He touched the grandeur all
     Men held of little worth.

He loved the growing flowers,
     The small bright singing birds,
The patient flocks of sheep,
     The many-pastured herds,

The field of rippling corn
     That shimmered in the sun,

The soft blue smoke of eve
     That curled when day was done . . .

He did not search a-far
     For what He had to say:
His mind reached forth and drew
     Its strength from every day:

The struggling nets, alive
     With fish drawn from the sea
Supplied Him with the apt
     And chosen simile. . . .

He saw a neighbor build
     A house that did not stand—
And men may not forget
     The House Upon The Sand;

He saw a widow drop
     Her mite into the hoard—
And to eternity
     That treasure up-stored;

He heard a publican
     Who thought none other there—
The souls of all mankind
     Are richer for that prayer. . . .

O, Poet of the World,
     I pray Thee, come to me,
That my lame heart might walk,
     That my dark soul may see;

And teach me, too, to go
     About the ways of earth
And find the wealth of God
     In things of little worth.

HARRY KEMP

❖❖❖

By a Carpenter mankind was made, and
only by that Carpenter can mankind be
remade.

DESIDERIUS ERASMUS

❖❖❖

BETHLEHEM OF BOAZ

Bethlehem of David,
 Of Ruth and Boaz' love,
Sweetly still you shining live
 Their fertile fields above.

"House of Bread" eternal,
 You nourish stalwart men,
While mothers in their homes of stone
 Toil with the strength of ten.

Far more than rubies are they worth.
 They fear not rain or snow.
They spin and weave and toiling, pray,
 As worthily they go.

The earth has many gentle towns,
 But just one Bethlehem.
Forever down the centuries,
 It wears love's diadem.

MADELEINE SWEENY MILLER

❖❖❖

JACOB'S WELL

Between Mount Ebal and Mount Gerizim,
 Where pass the caravans, lies Jacob's
  well,
Entrenched within a hoary past, Time's
  citadel.
  Here travelers slake their thirst from
   flowing brim
Of water-pots; maids gossip round its rim
 Of circling masonry. It casts a spell
That dims the Now and looses tongues to
  tell
  Of happenings of old, tales glad and
   grim.

One narrative forever hallows it,
 For here a woman of Samaria came
To fill her water jars. One sat there then
 Who spoke to her of living water, lit
The dormant spark within her soul to
  flame,
 Bade her to drink and never thirst
  again.

GEORGIA HARKNESS

❖❖❖

VISION AND FAITH

Christianity has no monopoly of hope. Jesus came into a world in which He found men already looking forward. What He brought was a clear vision of the goal, a reinforcement of the grounds for believing its attainment possible, and above all, the example of a faith which, faced with what seemed the certainty of failure, held steadfast and was justified by the event.

WILLIAM ADAMS BROWN

❖❖❖

CHRIST'S ANSWER

The gray hills taught me patience,
 The waters taught me prayer;
The flight of birds unfolded
 The marvel of Thy care!

The calm skies make me quiet,
 The high stars make me still;
The bolts of thunder teach me
 The lightning of Thy will!

Thy Soul is on the tempest,
 Thy Courage rides the air;
Through heaven and hell, I'll follow,
 I must—and so I dare!

ALLEN EASTMAN CROSS

❖❖❖

Be patient to live one day at a time as Jesus taught us, letting yesterday go and leaving tomorrow till it arrives.

JOSEPH FORT NEWTON

❖❖❖

God will never leave one whom He has chosen for His own.

CHARLES H. SPURGEON

❖❖❖

GOD'S OPTIMISM

Jesus never doubted. His vision was unclouded. His trust was absolute.

He saw God. He realized God. He hid Himself in God. In God He lived and moved and had His being.

He was no cheerful optimist who had shut His eyes to the sorrow and heartbreak of the world. Never were eyes wider open than His. He saw suffering in its every form.

He faces facts as they are and He predicts grander facts which are to be. He sees both sides—the bright side and the dark side—and having seen both sides His face has light on it. He felt the fury of the storm and was certain of the calm which was to follow. He could measure the dimensions of the night and also see the dawning of glorious morning.

His optimism was the optimism of God because He knew the secret of perfect trust.

W. A. CAMERON

❖❖❖

THE DEATHLESS TALE

Had He not breathed His breath
    Truly at Nazareth;
Had not His very feet
    Roamed many a hill and street;
Had Mary's story gone
    To time's oblivion;

Had the sweet record paled
    And the truth not prevailed;
Dormant and bleak had been
    This transitory scene,
And dark, thrice dark our earth
    Unknowing of His birth.

The flowers beheld His face,
    The stars knew His white grace.
The grass was greener for
    His humble stable door;

The rose upon its stem
    Redder for Bethlehem.

And we—are we not wise
    To cling with avid eyes
To the old tale, and be
    Moved by its memory?
Unutterably dim
    Our bright world, lacking Him.

CHARLES HANSON TOWNE

❖❖❖

MY LORD OF LITTLE BOATS

Some find their Lord on Calvary,
And some in bleak Gethsemane;
My trysting place is less remote—
I find Him by a little boat.

I seem to see His Presence glow
In ev'ry little boat I know,
And, as in far-off Galilee,
His voice comes calling, "Follow Me!"

He sat within a boat and taught,
And so each little ship is fraught
With sanctity of sea and sky
That holds a whispered, "It is I."

In any tranquil, harbored sail
I hear that Galilean gale!
The roar of waves and tempest shrill—
And then His calming, "Peace . . . be
    still."

A fishing boat, a net, an oar—
And there He watches on the shore,
His Spirit brooding o'er the sea,
To breathe a wistful, "Lov'st thou Me?"

Some find their Lord on mountain top,
And some in Joseph's busy shop—
I find Him where the shadows creep
By little boats that brave the deep.

BEATRICE PLUMB

❖❖❖

LOW TIDE

Make melody? Not I!
My soul lies flat and dry
As a sea beach under a sunless sky
When the tide is out.
Did I ever touch the strings
  Of poesy?
There is no voice in me
  That sings.
How the white waves leapt and sang
(And all the faery bells of music rang)
  When the tide was high!
Hardly my soul its lesson learns:
Does the dry sand doubt
  The sea
Till the tide turns?

ELEANOR PRESTON WATKINS

❖❖❖

TO EXPECT AND DESIRE

Remember that while you are seeking you
are also being sought. You will not be
lost, you will not miss the gate. You will
be found. You will be led. You will enter
in. Look for that. Expect it. Expect to
come to revelations of the Lord. Expect
shells to break in their season. Expect
boats to ride as the tide comes in.

This is hope, to desire and to expect.

To desire but not to expect is not hope,
for though you may desire the moon you
hardly hope for it.

To expect but not to desire is not hope,
for who that expects his loved one to die
could be said to hope for it?

But to desire, and to expect the desire's
fulfilment, that is hope.

And "we are saved by hope."

When hope is in the heart it is as prophetic as the song of a young stream on the
mountains. It is set for far destinies.

OSWALD W. S. MCCALL

❖❖❖

JESUS

Jesus, whose lot with us was cast,
  Who saw it out, from first to last:
Patient and fearless, tender, true,
  Carpenter, vagabond, felon, Jew:

Whose humorous eye took in each phase
  Of full, rich life this world displays,
Yet evermore kept fast in view
  The far-off goal it leads us to:

Who, as your hour neared, did not fail—
  The world's fate trembling in the
    scale—
With your half-hearted band to dine,
  And chat across the bread and wine:
Then went out firm to face the end,
  Alone, without a single friend:

Who felt, as your last words confessed,
  Wrung from a proud unflinching breast
By hours of dull ignoble pain,
  Your whole life's fight was fought in
    vain:
Would I could win and keep and feel
  That heart of love, that spirit of steel.

❖❖❖

THE POETS OF OLD ISRAEL

Old Israel's readers of the stars,
  I love them best. Musing, they read,
In embers of the heavenly hearth,
  High truths were never learned below.
They asked not of the barren sands,
  They questioned not that stretch of
    death;
But upward from the humble tent
  They took the stairway of the hills;
Upward they climbed, bold in their trust,
  To pluck the glory of the stars;
Faith falters, knowledge does not know,
  Fast, one by one, the phantoms fade;
But that strange light, unwavering love,
  Grasped from the lowered hand of God,
Abides, quenchless forevermore.

JOHN VANCE CHENEY

131

✥✥✥

THE BEST THINGS IN LIFE

The best and sweetest things in life are
   things you cannot buy:
The music of the birds at dawn, the
   rainbow in the sky;

The dazzling magic of the stars, the miracle of light;
The precious gifts of health and strength,
   of hearing, speech, and sight;

The peace of mind that crowns a busy
   life of work well done,
A faith in God that deepens as you face
   the setting sun;

The boon of love, the joy of friendship.
   As the years go by,
You find the greatest blessings are the
   things you cannot buy.

PATIENCE STRONG

✥✥✥

Those who kneel are bigger than those
who are standing, and those who bow
down stand up gigantic.

RAINER MARIA RILKE

✥✥✥

We bear the strain of earthly care,
   But bear it not alone.
Beside us walks our brother Christ,
   And makes our task His own.

The common hopes that make us men
   Were His in Galilee;
The tasks He gives are those He gave
   Beside the restless sea.

OZORA S. DAVIS

✥✥✥

INFLUENCE AND WITNESS

He never wrote a book, but more literature has been written about Him than any
other person.

He was not a musician, but His life
inspired the greater part of our immortal
music.

He was not an artist nor an architect,
but both of these arts achieved their finest
expression in the effort of men to honor
Him.

He was not a physician, but He probably healed the bodies and souls of more
men and women than the greatest of our
physicians. He has rightly been termed,
"The Great Physician."

He was not a king, a president, a dic-
tator, nor an official of any government,
but He accomplished more for the promotion of happiness, the assuaging of sorrow
and the promotion of justice and well-
being than any ruler or government in all
human history.

He wrote no songs, but He became the
theme of thousands of songs and choruses
that have come ringing down the centuries
and have spread hope and good will
around the world.

He never commanded an army, but
more volunteers enlisted under His banner
than any other.

No tyrant could control Him, Satan
failed to seduce Him and death could not
conquer Him. The grave failed to hold
Him. No wonder His birth divided the
centuries and His name stands above all
others.

With the coming of Jesus, the only
force that could blot out sin and create
newness of life entered the world. He came
that death might cease to have dominion
over us and, as He Himself said, that
we might have more abundant life. "I am
the Resurrection and the Life," He said.
"He that believeth in Me, though he were
dead, yet shall he live." This is our guar-
antee that death shall not hold dominion
over us and it is the brightest hope of
mankind.

Mount Hermon

. . . Jesus was transfigured before them

TRANSFIGURATION

❖❖❖

SCRIPTURE

Jesus taketh Peter, James, and John his brother, and bringeth them
up into an high mountain apart, and was transfigured before them:
and his face did shine as the sun, and his raiment was white as the
light. And, behold, there appeared unto them Moses and Elias
talking with him. Then answered Peter, and said unto Jesus, Lord, it
is good for us to be here: if thou wilt, let us make here three taber-
nacles; one for thee, and one for Moses, and one for Elias. While he
yet spake, behold, a bright cloud overshadowed them: and behold a
voice out of the cloud, which said, This is my beloved Son, in whom
I am well pleased; hear ye him. And when the disciples heard it, they
fell on their face, and were sore afraid. And Jesus came and touched
them, and said, Arise, and be not afraid. And when they had lifted
up their eyes, they saw no man, save Jesus only.

MATTHEW 17:1–8

And being found in fashion as a man, he humbled himself, and
became obedient unto death, even the death of the cross. Wherefore
God also hath highly exalted him, and given him a name which is
above every name: that at the name of Jesus every knee should bow,
of things in heaven, and things in earth, and things under the earth;
and that every tongue should confess that Jesus Christ is Lord, to the
glory of God the Father.

PHILIPPIANS 2:8–11

❖❖❖

MEDITATION

Rising more than 9000 feet, Mount Her-
mon, a twenty-mile ridge in northern Palestine, lay a short distance from Caesarea
Philippi where Peter declared his belief
in Christ's messiahship and Christ in response spoke of the necessity of His passion.

On the slope of this sacred mountain,
Jesus and three of His disciples went to
pray. Before the amazed disciples the appearance of Jesus was changed—"the fashion of his countenance," Luke records,

"was altered"—and the inner beauty and
nature of the Son of God was manifested.

In a vision the disciples beheld Moses
and Elijah, a testimony that Christ was the
fulfillment of both law and prophecy.

The Transfiguration, coming at this
crucial hour in Christ's life, authenticated
His divine mission. It foreshadowed His
Lordship which, as He said, would be
complete and convincing following His
resurrection and ascension when He sat
at the right hand of God.

TRANSFIGURATION

Transfigured on a mount the Master
    stood,
  His raiment white, and dazzling to the
    sight
In radiance divine. It would be good
  To stay and dwell forever in that light,
So Peter thought—but Jesus spake him
    nay.
  He knew that all about was work to do,
That in the vale below a sick boy lay,
  And troubled folk they might bring
    healing to.

I too have seen a vision on a mount—
  Have gazed on dazzling whiteness, and
    been swept
By mountain winds, dew-cleansed at morn-
    ing's fount.
  I yearned to linger there—but down-
    ward crept
A mist, and drove me to the vale below.
  Because He went, I was less loath to go.

GEORGIA HARKNESS

❖❖❖

The purpose of the transfiguration has been variously stated, such as to establish Jesus as the Messiah, to confirm the status of Jesus in the presence of the laws and the prophets, to nerve and strengthen Jesus for the terrible ordeal ahead of Him, and to reconcile His men to the approaching violence by revealing to them the glory that should follow. One wonders whether the real reason for the transfiguration is not stated for us so casually by St. Luke that, with the dramatic happenings described immediately, and in the midst of the pageantry, we miss his remark. It is that "Jesus went into the mountain to pray."

GEORGE ARTHUR CLARKE

❖❖❖

Of course we long to be more than we are because we are more than we are.

MARGUERITTE HARMON BRO

❖❖❖

HORIZON

Jesus lived life in its wholeness. He essayed the heights. He did not shrink from the depths.

Three years, they say, He lived before men, yet in that time He managed to let eternity break through, and lifted man's horizon to infinity.

He took all that came to Him, and turned it to the purpose of His mission, circumstance, failure, disappointment, and death.

They gave Him a manger for a cradle, a bench for a pulpit, thorns for a crown, and a cross for a throne; but He took them and made them the very glory of His career.

He turned sorrow into joy, He found strength in labor, peace in the storm, rest on the cross, and life in the grave.

WILLIAM E. ORCHARD

❖❖❖

Jesus was a new star in the firmament of religious teachers. His character was so majestic that many followed Him and memorized His sayings. Yet always He stood upon the Scriptures.

You and I dwell in magnificent company when we study the Bible and submit to its authority. We stand with Christ.

And our ranks are swelled by Augustine, Huss, Tyndale, Wycliffe, Luther, Calvin, Wesley, and a host of others.

We give thanks for the Scriptures. May it yet be said of us, as the heavenly Christ said of the church in ancient Philadelphia, "For thou hast a little strength, and hast kept my word, and hast not denied my name."

HARRY B. SCHULTHEIS

A DOOR WIDE OPEN

His is a life that bubbled up copiously from unknown inward deeps.

Whenever it meets with obstacles, this life simply streams by them or cuts a channel for itself through them. It is not checked or diverted from its course.

The impetus of its power never seems to ebb. Not one whit of personal desire found welcome in His heart. But the desire of God for the world was treated like the royal guest it is.

The only life that He would accept for Himself was the one set for Him by the will of God; He asked no other.

He fixed upon no goal for Himself, adopted no resolution of His own devising, selected no wish of His own to realize; but from hour to hour He simply adopted deed after deed and word after word as they were announced to Him out of the will of God.

For once in the history of mankind the will universal found the door wide open by which to enter in its full purity into a human being.

And so there resounds through everything Jesus does and says something that seems to come from the deepest recesses of the mystery of the world itself.

FRIEDRICH RITTELMEYER

❖❖❖

COMPANY OF FAITH

The first impression that the new reading of the Book of Acts has made upon me is of the extraordinary adequacy of the persons spoken of in it for their quite impossible task.

They were quite ordinary people. There wasn't an able man among them, certainly not a learned man, not a scholar, not a public man, not a leading business man. They were just fisher-folk and peasants and the like.

If you had chanced in upon their meeting in the Upper Room, I imagine you wouldn't have thought much of it. You would have seen a company of rather forlorn and bewildered men and women, nursing a rather mysterious hope to which they couldn't give a name, and which, therefore, you would regard as negligible and unimportant.

And yet that company had its moment and that moment, that experience on the Day of Pentecost, transfigured them, lifted them to such a pitch of power that at their word thousands were won over to them. Weak men became fearless leaders. Nonentities grew into strong generative giants.

Their souls took on an unheard-of stature and things happened at the word and the deed of these men that break through the ordinary frontiers of experience.

RICHARD ROBERTS

❖❖❖

THE YOUNG MESSIAH

His brothers gaze at him with puzzled
    eyes.
    He is their own—He has the selfsame
      blood;
And yet He dreams that once in Paradise
    He walked with God beside a silver
      flood.
He's in the City of Jerusalem
    With streets of gold and walls of precious
      stone.
Tall lilies line the river, stem to stem,
    And there's a tree with branches blossom-
      blown.

The past He carries with Him, to and fro,
    Along the paths the many years have
      made.
The present mingles with the long ago
    As faring feet into the Jordan wade.
He dares the desert, braves its burning
    breath—
    The One of Heaven now of Nazareth!

LESLIE CLARE MANCHESTER

ECCE HOMO

He too saw sunshine filter through the
    trees
  And watched the sunbeams dance in
    secret ways;
Heard vagrant voices in the scented breeze
  Mocking the moonmist's fleeting ecsta-
    sies.

He too saw somber shadows slowly shroud
  With velvet-dust the drowsy, dying day;
Heard January winds wail low and loud,
  And watched the leafless lindens gently
    sway.

He too felt sad when flowers shut up at
    nights.
  And hollow-sounding footfalls filled the
    air;
But spellbound when upon the holy heights
  He knelt, 'mid trumpet-moss, in private
    prayer.

JOHNSTONE G. PATRICK

✥✥✥

God does not make the mountain tops to be
inhabited. They are not for the homes of
men. We ascend the height to catch a
broader vision of our earthly surroundings,
but we do not tarry there. We descend to
our farms, our shops, our studies, our household tasks. This need not be a downfall. Let
life hold its true meaning and all duty
becomes sacred.

HENRY DRUMMOND

✥✥✥

DERIVED LIFE

The initiative is always His. In every beginning God. Not only is He behind and in
the cosmos—its originating mind, its sustaining life, its manifest beauty—but if we
know anything about Him, it is not because
men boldly investigated and ferreted out
this elusive spirit. He has always been
revealing Himself.

Jeremiah graphically reports God as saying: "I spake unto you, rising up early and
speaking." Men who were waiting listened
and heard. Hence, the Bible and other
divine words through the centuries.

If we listen, a contemporary word comes
to us from these utterances of long ago
and in the events of today.

The central fact in the Christian heritage
is a figure, a Man who lived by faith, who
waited on His Father. But He did not think
of Himself as originating anything. He
spoke of Himself as one sent. His was a
derived life. His work was a mission from
above.

HENRY SLOANE COFFIN

✥✥✥

THE PARTING

That He might better of Love's mystery
    tell
  Into a lonely mountain they withdrew,
Day's golden fire cooled in deep wells of
    dew
  About His Head with softened splendor
    fell;
And in each heart that heard the last
    farewell
  A quickening joy and deepening sorrow
    grew,
And all were hushed—even the doubtful
    knew
  His was the power of Heaven and of
    Hell.

When He had ceased, a mighty wind rushed
    by
  From far beyond the sunset's cloudless
    rim,
And over them a glory seemed to bend;
  Then like a star He rose into the sky,
Sadly they watched the glowing light grow
    dim
  And heard the echoes ring, "Until the
    End."

THOMAS S. JONES, JR.

138

RENEWAL

In trouble then and fear I sought
   The Man who taught in Galilee;
And peace unto my soul was brought,
   And all my faith came back to me.

❖❖❖

THE HUNGRY

Whom does He love the most—
   The poor, the sick, the blind,
The rich, the maimed, the host
   Unknowingly unkind?

The ones who strive, and fail;
   The ones who have, and lose;
The ones who will not quail
   Nor martyrdom refuse?

The wind went sobbing low
   To His great Heart and cried:
"Dear God, they need you so,—
   Who die unsatisfied."

CAROLINE GILTINAN

❖❖❖

DIVINE LODESTONE

When the first spark of a desire after God arises in thy soul, cherish it with all thy care, give all thy heart unto it.

It is nothing less than a touch of the divine Lodestone that is to draw thee out of the vanity of time into the riches of eternity.

Get up, therefore, and follow it as gladly as the wise men of the East followed the star from heaven that appeared to them.

It will do for thee as the star did for them: it will lead thee to the birth of Jesus, not in a stable at Bethlehem of Judaea, but to the birth of Jesus in the dark center of thine own fallen soul.

WILLIAM LAW

❖❖❖

MOUNTAIN VISION

Remember that vision on the Mount of Transfiguration, and let it be ours, even in the glare of earthly joys and brightness, to lift up our eyes, like those wondering three, and see no man any more save Jesus only.

ALEXANDER MACLAREN

❖❖❖

We are always becoming Christians.

SØREN KIERKEGAARD

❖❖❖

Great things are done when men and mountains meet.

WILLIAM BLAKE

❖❖❖

ADORATION

Adoration is the first and greatest of life's responses to its spiritual environment; the first and most fundamental of spirit's movements toward Spirit; the seed from which all other prayer must spring.

It is among the most powerful of the educative forces which purify the understanding, form and develop the spiritual life.

As we can never know the secret of great art or music until we have learned to look and listen with a self-oblivious reverence, acknowledging a beauty that is beyond our grasp—so the claim and loveliness of God remain unrealized, till we have learned to look, to listen, to adore.

Then only do we go beyond ourselves and our small vision, pour ourselves out to that which we know not, and so escape from our own pettiness and limitation into the universal life.

EVELYN UNDERHILL

Jaffa

. . . workers together with God

WORK

✤✤✤

SCRIPTURE

Let the beauty of the Lord our God be upon us: and establish thou the work of our hands upon us; yea, the work of our hands establish thou it.

PSALM 90:17

Is not this the carpenter, the son of Mary, the brother of James, and Joses, and of Juda, and Simon?

MARK 6:3

So he that had received five talents came and brought other five talents, saying, Lord, thou deliveredst unto me five talents: behold, I have gained beside them five talents more. His Lord said unto him, Well done, thou good and faithful servant: thou hast been faithful over a few things, I will make thee ruler over many things: enter thou into the joy of thy lord.

MATTHEW 25:20–21

Then saith he unto his disciples, The harvest truly is plenteous, but the labourers are few; pray ye therefore the Lord of the harvest, that he will send forth labourers into his harvest.

MATTHEW 9:37–38

✤✤✤

MEDITATION

Work was structured into the life of man in the story of the Creation: "the Lord God took the man and put him into the garden of Eden to dress it and keep it." God set apart six days for labor and the seventh day for rest.

Although work has been considered by some to be a curse pronounced upon man because of Adam's disobedience, most people have found work to be a blessing and a source of both fulfillment and dignity.

The Carpenter of Nazareth commended work by His example, as did the Apostle Paul, who by trade was a tentmaker. Paul gave to work a sacramental character when he wrote to the Christians in the Church at Corinth that "we are labourers together with God."

Christian history has approved the privilege and disciplines of work, considering all worthy effort to be a divine calling.

Joppa, a Mediterranean seaport for more than thirty-five centuries and the avenue to the sea for Jerusalem, typifies work, for there Simon, a tanner by trade, provided a room for Simon Peter, and there, too, Peter's prayers restored life to a charitable Christian disciple named Dorcas, who "was full of good works and almsdeeds" and known for the coats and garments which she made.

CARPENTER CHRIST

Carpenter Christ, I know that you must understand. I praise You most for work.

Surely hands that stripped the cedar bough in Nazareth must be akin to hands that love the homely touch of bread.

Surely fingers that had no fear to heal the leper must know the joy of menial tasks to rest a weary one.

And eyes that watched a passion flower triumphant on a barren hill must live again to see the ecstasy of every loving bloom.

Carpenter Christ!

MILDRED FOWLER FIELD

INCARNATION

Jesus was God in a carpenter's apron, wielding a mallet and chisel, or God in friendship and conversation, God with helping hands.

HAROLD E. KOHN

THE CARPENTER

Silent at Joseph's side He stood,
    And smoothed and trimmed the shapeless wood.
And with firm hand, assured and slow,
    Drove in each nail with measured blow.

Absorbed, He planned a wooden cask,
    Nor asked for any greater task.
Content to make, with humble tools,
    Tables and little children's stools.

Lord, give me careful hands to make
    Such simple things as for Thy sake.
Happy within Thine House to dwell
    If I may make one table well.

PHYLLIS HARTNOLL

CALL FOR WORKERS

The lazy and idle seldom hear the call of God. It is often when intent on some useful work and while pursuing a helpful calling that God's voice is heard. Here are a few examples from the Bible:

Moses was busy with his flock at Horeb.

Gideon was busy threshing wheat by the wine press.

Saul was busy searching for his father's lost beasts.

Elisha was busy plowing with twelve yoke of oxen.

David was busy caring for his father's sheep.

Nehemiah was busy bearing the king's wine-cup.

Amos was busy caring for his sheep and sycamore fruit and attending the market.

Peter and Andrew were busy casting their nets into the sea.

Lydia was busy preparing and selling her purple fabrics.

James and John were busy mending their nets.

Matthew was busy collecting customs duties.

Mary and Elizabeth were busy with their homemaking.

Jesus was busy probably in the carpenter shop and about His Father's business.

SOUL BUILDING

While Jesus was interested in doing His work, He was undoubtedly more interested in the human beings about Him and in their development.

As He went about His job of contracting for buildings or whatever His task may have been, He recognized that the great thing to be done in this world was the construction, the building of the soul of humanity.

ARTHUR NASH

THE COMPANION

Here in my workshop where I toil
  Till head and hands are well-nigh spent;
Out on the road where the dust and soil
  Fall thick on garments worn and rent;
Or in the kitchen where I bake
  The bread the little children eat—
He comes, His hand of strength I take,
  And every lonely task grows sweet.

❖❖❖

DIVINE WORKER

Jesus Christ was a workingman.

His hands were fitted to labor as His voice was fitted to music.

He entered into the condition of the great majority of mankind and became one of them in the fellowship of toil, and from that time it has been hard for a man to get into better company than that of working people.

GEORGE HALL

❖❖❖

WORK AND WORSHIP

Work and worship correspond to two great primary needs of human nature. They are not antagonistic but complementary.

Prayer recalls us from the mere instrumental agencies of life to life itself, from the outward to the inward, from the fragmentary to the idea of the whole.

Hence work without prayer tends to make us strangers to ourselves.

We are lost in our activities; they become dull drudgeries, and we need to discover ourselves afresh. But this self-discovery implies the discovery of God as the object and measure and meaning of existence.

Just as sleep and food replenish the exhausted energies of the body, so prayer —the return to the Spirit of our spirits— renews the powers of the soul, giving back to them poise and momentum.

Other things being equal, the praying man is more efficient, physically, mentally, and spiritually, than the non-praying man.

His mind works freely, unclouded by passion; his nervous power is not fretted by waste and worry. He is more potent in the battle of life.

The vision of what it all means, its divine and eternal significance, endows him with new resolve to fling himself without reserve into the task committed to him, to suffer what must be endured, not as a blind stroke of fate but as an opportunity for the display of new and unsuspected capacity.

SAMUEL MC COMB

❖❖❖

JESUS THE CARPENTER

If I could hold within my hand
  The hammer Jesus swung,
Not all the gold in all the land,
Nor jewels countless as the sand,
  All in the balance flung,
Could weigh the value of that thing
Round which His fingers once did cling.

If I could have the table Christ
  Once made in Nazareth,
Not all the pearls in all the sea,
Nor crowns of kings or kings to be
  As long as men have breath,
Could buy that thing of wood He made—
The Lord of Lords who learned a trade.

Yea, but His hammer still is shown
  By honest hands that toil,
And round His table men sit down;
And all are equals, with a crown
  Nor gold nor pearls can soil;
The shop of Nazareth was bare—
But brotherhood was builded there.

CHARLES M. SHELDON

❖❖❖

THE CARPENTER

This He was then—
  A workman among working men.

He knew the orchards of Gennesaret;
  The circled vineyards that were set
Like living cinctures, branch and root,
  And jeweled with their purple fruit.
The somber olives, wide of limb,
  Had sheltered Him
At noontide, when He had to pass
  Beneath a sky of shimmering brass.
He knew the almond trees, that spread
  Frail rosy clouds above His head;
The groves of oak and terebinth,
  And where the fruit of colocynth
Ran tangled through the scarlet fires
  Of lilies and anemones,
And where, above the walnut trees,
  The tall firs lifted pointed spires.

He knew the miracle of night; the throb-
  bing gold
  Of eastern stars, merging in wistful rose
Of day, that lingers here as though to hold
  The blended glories, and reluctant, goes
Down the wide hills at last, and toward
  the sea;
    These things He knew, and all the
    majesty
Of planets set on height ascending height—
  Vistas and terraces of light;
As though divided by a single breath,
  Were God—and Nazareth.

Here were no dark misgivings, and no
  doubt.
  All night He lived a greater prayer than
  words,
Until the dawn He saw the fishing-fleets
  go out
  Like a low flight of birds.
He watched the hillslopes lightly sprayed
  with gold;

He saw the sheep come bleating from
  the fold,
And in the air, a lark.
  While down the road, between the hills
  at last,
With tinkling bells, a train of camels
  passed.
  With rhythmic steps, He saw them go
Upon their way to Jericho,
  And in His shop, He knew, were good,
Red cedar boards and olive wood,
  Where waiting for His fingers, were
The labors of a carpenter.

A night of stars and God—and then
  A workman's toil with working men.

MARY BRENT WHITESIDE

❖❖❖

One thing, and only one, in this world has eternity stamped upon it. Feelings pass, resolves and thoughts pass, and opinions change. What you have done lasts—lasts to you. Through ages, through eternity, what you have done for Christ, that, and only that, you are.

FREDERICK W. ROBERTSON

❖❖❖

PANORAMA OF PROGRESS

There is no such thing as an insignificant job. If the small tasks are left undone, there can be little hope that the larger ones will be achieved.

All work is a part of the panorama of progress. No task, however humble, is to be considered unimportant.

Without the acorn there can be no oak. Without the ditchdigger there can be no skyscraper.

So long as the ditchdigger has visions of the cathedral he is building, his work will, to him, remain great.

LEO BENNETT

❖❖❖

146

CARPENTER

He sang at His bench in Nazareth
   While His strong young hands took
     hold
Of plank and nail to broaden the door
   For a shepherd neighbor's fold.

Into His hands on Calvary
   He took the nails again
To make the door which leads to God
   Wide for His fellow men.

LESLIE SAVAGE CLARK

❖❖❖

PORTRAIT

Jesus was the poorest man who ever walked the dirt roads of earth. Born in poverty and reared in obscurity, He yet lived to enrich mankind. A stable was His birthplace, a manger His cradle. For twenty years He worked as a carpenter in a poverty-stricken and despised village which bore the scorn of men as they asked, "Can any good thing come out of Nazareth?"

He began His ministry at the Jordan River, with no organization to support Him, no patrons to enrich Him. He publicly began a life of poverty that ended at the tomb. He preached without price, and wrought miracles without money. As far as we know, He never possessed the value of one dollar. How pathetic His words, "The foxes have holes and the birds of the air their nests, but the Son of Man hath not where to lay his head."

He was an itinerant preacher whose parish was the world. When invited, He entered men's homes for dinner. When unasked, He went hungry. He sought breakfast from the leafing fig tree, but found none. He ate grain from His hands as He walked through fields of corn. His support came from the gifts of a few women, and His treasurer stole part of the pittance put therein. He walked over the hills of Judea and by the waters of Galilee enriching men, Himself the poorest of all. He slept often under the open sky, in the wilderness without food, by Jacob's well without water, in the crowded city without a home. Thus He lived and loved, toiled and died. His value was thirty pieces of silver when sold—the price of a slave, the lowest estimate of human life.

So poor was He that He needs must carry His own cross through the city until, fainting, he fell. In a potter's field, He was nailed to that cross between two thieves, stripped of His robe, the gift of love, for which inhuman soldiers gambled as He died. With no estate with which to endow His weeping and widowed mother, He bequeathed her to the love of the beloved John. Then He gave His peace to the disciples, His pardon to the thief, His life for the world, His body to the cross, and His spirit to God. His burial clothes were the gift of a friend. He was laid at last in a borrowed grave.

Truly, Jesus Christ was the poorest man that ever walked the dirt roads of earth. Though He was rich, yet for our sakes He became poor, that we, through His poverty, might become rich.

THE TREASURY OF INSPIRATIONAL
ANECDOTES

❖❖❖

QUALITY

Place special emphasis upon the quality of your work.

When the chief aim of your daily life is to produce intrinsically the best and not merely the outwardly attractive, you can then afford to disregard the approval and praise of men.

The inner consciousness of work worthily attempted and well done is its own reward.

GRENVILLE KLEISER

❖❖❖

WORK

Close by the careless worker's side
　　Still patient stands
The Carpenter of Nazareth,
　　With pierced hands
Outstretched to plead unceasingly
　　His Love's demands.

Longing to pick the hammer up
　　And strike a blow,
Longing to feel His plane swing out,
　　Steady and slow,
The fragrant shavings falling down,
　　Silent as snow.

Because this is my work, O Lord,
　　It must be Thine,
Because it is a human task
　　It is divine.
Take me, and brand me with Thy cross,
　　Thy slave's proud sign.

　　　　　　　G. A. STUDDERT-KENNEDY

❖❖❖

LIFE GAVE ME THESE

These are the gifts life gave to me:
A wide green lawn and an old oak tree,
A sheltering roof to cover my head,
Pleasant dreams and a restful bed—

Joys of the season: the breath of spring,
Autumn's wonder at teal-tipped wing,
Lushness of summer in leaf and flower,
The snow-etched church at the Sabbath
　　hour—

A constant man who through the years
Has guided his loved ones through faith
　　and fears,
Mirth and laughter, a daughter's song . . .
All these to treasure my whole life long.

Lord, give me the grace and taste to won-
　　der . . .
Rain comes best with the muted thunder.

　　　　　　　ZELLA G. WALLACE

❖❖❖

GIFT OF CREATIVITY

We must ever keep in mind the ruling idea that each one of us is made in the image of God.

This means that we are made to be creators, because God is the Creator of all. At one point in creation God has shared the gift of creativity.

This is why we are never really happy unless we are *making*.

The greatest happiness comes in the kind of life in which we clearly leave the world different from what it was when we began.

To make a home, to write an essay, to build a factory, to establish a church—these are acts that make men sing.

　　　　　　　ELTON TRUEBLOOD

❖❖❖

PRAYER

O Son of Man, Thou madest known,
　　Through quiet work in shop and home,
The sacredness of common things,
　　The chance of life that each day brings.

O Workman true, may we fulfill,
　　In daily life the Father's will;
In duty's call, Thy call we hear
　　To fuller life through work sincere.

Thou Master Workman, grant us grace
　　The challenge of our tasks to face;
By loyal scorn of second best,
　　By effort true, to meet each test.

And thus we pray in deed and word,
　　Thy kingdom come on earth, O Lord;
In work that gives effect to prayer
　　Thy purpose for Thy world we share.

　　　　　　　MILTON S. LITTLEFIELD

❖❖❖

THE CARPENTER'S SON

I know He must have loved the smell of
  wood,
  The sight of shavings curling from the
    plane,
The endless curves and blendings of the
  grain
  Tracing a pattern suited to each mood;
I think He visioned how the tree had stood
  Through years of winter snow and sum-
    mer rain
On some sharp mountain slope or wooded
  plain
  Awaiting its career as home—or rood.
So that at last, when all His world went
  black
  And trust in man trembled with every
    stroke
That drove the nails and pierced Him with
  the lack
  Of loyal friends to share His heavy yoke,
I think He must have loved along His back
  The honest strength and fortitude of oak.

EDWIN O. KENNEDY

❖❖❖

THE DAY AND THE WORK

There is waiting a work where only his
  hands can avail;
And so, if he falters, a chord in the music
  will fail.
He may laugh to the sky, he may lie for an
  hour in the sun;
But he dare not go hence till the labor
  appointed is done.

To each man is given a marble to carve
  for the wall:
A stone that is needed to heighten the
  beauty of all;
And only his soul has the magic to give
  it a grace,
And only his hands have the cunning to
  put it in place.

EDWIN MARKHAM

❖❖❖

WORK IN LOVE

Our Lord does not care
so much for the importance
of our works as
for the love with which they are done.

TERESA OF AVILA

❖❖❖

A TEACHER'S PSALM

The Lord is my Teacher;
  I shall not lose the way to wisdom.
He leadeth me in the lowly path of learning.
  He prepareth a lesson for me every day,
He findeth the clear fountain of instruc-
  tion—
  Little by little He showeth me the beauty
    of truth.

The world is a great book that He has
  written,
  He turneth the leaves for me slowly;
They are all inscribed with images and
  letters—
  His voice poureth light on the pictures
    and the words.

Then am I glad when I perceive His mean-
  ing.
  He taketh me by the hand to the hill-top
    of wisdom;
In the valley, also, He walketh beside me,
  And in the dark places He whispereth in
    my heart.

Yea, though my lesson be hard, it is not
  hopeless,
  For the Lord is very patient with His
    slow scholar.
He will wait awhile for my weakness—
  He will help me to read the truth
    through tears—
Surely Thou wilt enlighten me daily by joy
  and by sorrow,
  And lead me at last, O Lord, to the per-
    fect knowledge of Thee.

HENRY VAN DYKE

Jerusalem

. . . light from the Upper Room

COMMUNION

❖❖❖

SCRIPTURE

When the hour was come, he sat down, and the twelve apostles with him. And he said unto them, With desire I have desired to eat this passover with you before I suffer: for I say unto you, I will not any more eat thereof, until it be fulfilled in the kingdom of God. And he took the cup, and gave thanks, and said, Take this, and divide it among yourselves: for I say unto you, I will not drink of the fruit of the vine, until the kingdom of God shall come. And he took bread, and gave thanks, and brake it, and gave unto them, saying, This is my body which is given for you: this do in remembrance of me. Likewise also the cup after supper, saying, This cup is the new testament in my blood, which is shed for you.

LUKE 22:14–20

Let a man examine himself, and so let him eat of that bread, and drink of that cup.

I CORINTHIANS 11:28

The cup of blessing which we bless, is it not the communion of the blood of Christ? The bread which we break, is it not the communion of the body of Christ? For we being many are one bread, and one body: for we are all partakers of that one bread.

I CORINTHIANS 10:16–17

❖❖❖

MEDITATION

Holy Communion recalls the evening when Jesus and His disciples gathered in a "large upper room" in Jerusalem to observe the Passover, the deliverance of the Jews from Egyptian bondage.

The apostolic company climbed to the upper room by an outside staircase. During the meal Jesus gave to His friends cakes of unleavened bread representative of His body to be broken on Calvary and also a cup of wine to symbolize His sacrificial death.

For all Christians, however variously the sacrament is commemorated, the Lord's Supper is "the common meal" in which remembrance is rekindled, thanksgiving is offered, Christ's return—"till he come"—is anticipated, and the world-wide unity of the Church of Christ is affirmed.

The spirit of this "communion of the blood and body of Christ" is sensitively expressed in Horatius Bonar's hymn:

Here, O my Lord, I see Thee face to face;
Here would I touch and handle things unseen;
Here grasp with firmer hand eternal grace,
And all my weariness upon Thee lean.

153

❧❧❧

The Holy Communion is an extension of the stable at Bethlehem, the shop at Nazareth, the miracles of the seashore, the teachings of the hillside, the agony of the cross, and the radiance of resurrection.

S. S. DRURY

❧❧❧

ROOM OF MEMORIES

It is small wonder that this upper room has been a dearer place to Christendom than all the great cathedrals raised by subsequent ages to Jesus' honor.

Its story was not finished when the Master rose from the table there and led His friends out to Gethsemane; it was not finished when the candles were extinguished that night and silence reigned again.

For when after Calvary the broken-hearted, leaderless disciples sought a hiding place and refuge from the threatening mob, it was in this same upper room that they found it.

This was the place which witnessed their hopeless mourning for the Master they had lost; and this was the place where that mourning was turned to bewildered, incredulous joy when Jesus came back to them through the closed and bolted door, and revealed Himself risen and alive (John 20:19).

Here, too, it is more than likely, they gathered again when He had ascended to His Father; and here the Spirit fell, flooding their souls with the glory of Pentecost and giving birth to the Christian Church (Acts 1:13, 2:1).

If the tradition is correct which identifies this upper room with the house in Jerusalem to which Peter made his way on his escape from prison (Acts 12:12), we should be able to conclude that the "goodman of the house," who figures so mysteriously in the Gospel story (Mark 14:14), was none

other than the husband of Mary, the mother of John Mark, the earliest evangelist.

The "certain young man" who according to Mark's Gospel was present in Gethsemane and escaped with difficulty when Jesus was arrested may have been Mark himself (Mark 14:51).

We can imagine him helping his father and mother to prepare the upper room for Jesus and His friends, waiting outside the door while the Last Supper was celebrated that night, and then following the little group out to the garden on Olivet to see what was to happen.

Be that as it may, this upper room of many memories will always draw and hold the hearts of Christ's people wherever the Gospel is preached; and every time the bread of our Communion is broken and the wine poured out, we feel that we are meeting with Jesus there.

JAMES S. STEWART

❧❧❧

TWO CHALICES

There was a chalice in the ancient East
  Unhallowed by the Master of the Feast;
It did not catch the sacramental tide
  That welled from Jesus' lacerated side,
Nor lure Sir Galahad to seek the shrine
  Whence glowed its radiance and flowed
    its wine.
It was abandoned at a village well
  When once a passing stranger stopped
    to tell
Of founts of living water that may spring
  Within the soul, and make the spirit sing.

Two sacred chalices I shall acclaim:
  One from an upper room; of lesser fame
One from a well, illumined by His name.

EDWIN MC NEILL POTEAT

❧❧❧

154

THE SACRAMENT

"This is my body, which is given for you;
　　Do this," He said, "and break, remem-
　　　b'ring me."
O Lamb of God, our Paschal off'ring true,
　　To us the Bread of Life each moment be.

"This is my blood, for sins' remission shed";
　　He spake, and passed the cup of blessing
　　　round;
So let us drink, and, on life's fullness fed,
　　With heavenly joy each quickening pulse
　　　shall bound.

Some will betray thee—"Master, is it I?"
　　Leaning upon Thy love, we ask in fear—
Ourselves mistrusting, earnestly we cry
　　To Thee, the Strong, for strength, when
　　　sin is near.

But round us fall the evening shadows dim;
　　A saddened awe pervades our darkening
　　　sense;
In solemn choir we sing the parting hymn,
　　And hear Thy voice, "Arise, let us go
　　　hence."

CHARLES L. FORD

❖❖❖

PRAYER

Lord, this is Thy feast, prepared by Thy
longing, spread at Thy command, attended
at Thine invitation, blessed by Thine own
word, distributed by Thine own hand, the
undying memorial of Thy sacrifice upon
the cross, the full gift of Thine everlasting
love, and its perpetuation till time shall
end.

　Lord, this is Bread of heaven, Bread of
life, that whoso eateth never shall hunger
more. And this the Cup of pardon, healing,
gladness, strength, that whoso drinketh,
thirsteth not again. So may we come, O
Lord, to Thy table; Lord Jesus, come to
us.

OLIVE WYON

❖❖❖

A PILGRIM IN PALESTINE

When I go to Bethlehem
　　And in the straw-strewn stable linger,
A little Babe lifts up His hand
　　And tries to grasp my finger.

When I visit Nazareth
　　And climb the hill to view the land,
An eager Boy runs up the path
　　And takes me by the hand.

When I walk in Galilee
　　And all the storied places find,
I meet a Man at every turn
　　Whose words possess my mind.

When I kneel at Calvary
　　Ere from this sacred land depart,
A Presence close beside me comes
　　Who warms and claims my heart.

MERLO HEICHER

❖❖❖

SECRET OF LIFE

To give one's life away to what one knows
to be of highest worth, not only for oneself,
but for all mankind, is the most mature
experience open to man. It can help him
face death and tragedy undismayed. It possesses the secret of life everlasting.

GREGORY VLASTOS

❖❖❖

If we show the Lord's death at Communion,
we must show the Lord's life in this world.
If it is a Eucharist on Sunday, it must
prove on Monday that it was also a Sacrament.

MALTBIE D. BABCOCK

❖❖❖

REMEMBRANCE

The sun lay warm on tawny fields
  Of wheat in Galilee,
Where lilies swayed and winds were soft
  Beside a summer sea.

There purple vineyards climbed the slopes
  And fragrance filled the air,
While flocks of doves on silver wings
  Ascended like a prayer.

Was He, perhaps, remembering
  The peace of wheat and vine
That night He made a sacrament
  Of bread and wine?

LESLIE SAVAGE CLARK

❖❖❖

No apostle, no New Testament writer, ever
remembered Christ. The Christian religion
depends not on what Christ was, merely;
but on what He is, not simply on what
He did, but on what He does.

JAMES DENNEY

❖❖❖

ON FINDING JESUS

The Jesus whom you have received into
your hearts in your Communion is the same
Jesus who is enshrined in the hearts of
His brothers and sisters in the world.

Now go and look for Jesus in those who
have lost hope, in those who are struggling
to make good.

Look for Jesus in them, and when you
find Him, gird yourselves with His towel
of fellowship and with His feet in the person of His brethren.

BROOKE F. WESTCOTT

❖❖❖

WORDS ON THE WIND

The white-robed separation
Of Jesus on a stone-arched street,
And the people blindly laying branches
Underneath a donkey's feet,
Come strangely to our modern hearing,
And time has veiled His village birth;
But His words blow from a windy hillside
Out across the purple Earth,
With echoes never dying
In the multitude still crying
For a God that we can meet.

MANFRED A. CARTER

❖❖❖

The Holy Supper is kept, indeed,
  In whatso we share with another's need;
Not what we give, but what we share,
  For the gift without the giver is bare;
Who gives himself with his alms feeds three,
  Himself, his hungering neighbor, and
  Me.

JAMES RUSSELL LOWELL

❖❖❖

MEDITATION FOR HOLY COMMUNION

At twilight hour the burdened Savior came
With His disciples to the upper room.
The feast was spread, soft-lit by oil lamp's
  flame.
Each sensed the presence of impending
  doom.
"This is my body; take, and eat," He said;
"And drink the cup; my blood for you
  outpoured."
And as they ate and drank, their hearts He
  read
And found not one to Him securely
  moored:
One would betray, another would deny,
And one escape from dark Gethsemane;
And one, unsure of self, said, "Is it I?"
The unpossessed of Christ thus never see!
Possess us, Lord, for otherwise we're lost;
Infuse Thyself with us at Pentecost!

RUSSELL Q. CHILCOTE

HOLY GROUND

To that upper room of long ago and far away, that quiet sanctuary amid the clash and clamor of the world, the heart of Christendom continually returns. Here, if anywhere, is holy ground.

JAMES S. STEWART

THE UPPER ROOM

They waited in the old, familiar place—
    The upper room—sacred to memory—
The Master's friends, who shuddered now
        to face
    Cross-shadowed days to come, and hope-
        lessly,
Their voices hushed, and heads bowed low
        in grief,
    With hearts that beat a never-ceasing cry,
From depths that held despair beyond
        belief,
    They flung their doubt to the unan-
        swered "Why?"

They waited . . . while His Spirit touched
        them there—
    A living flame of courage, vision's breath,
That annihilation never knows, and where
    Crumbles to dust the vanquished power
        of death.

We, who have lost so much—disconsolate—
    Let us go to the upper room . . . and
        wait.

IDA NORTON MUNSON

I am convinced that the universe is under the control of a loving purpose and that in the struggle for righteousness man has cosmic companionship. Behind the harsh appearances of the world there is a benign power. God is a living God.

MARTIN LUTHER KING, JR.

THE BREAD OF LIFE

E'er I set forth upon this day,
    Break Thou to me Thy bread,
Pour forth Thy strengthening, dear Lord,
    In gladness o'er my head.

Yea, grant my faint and hungry heart
    Thy food from heaven above;
O come, Thou living Bread of Life,
    Reveal Thy gifts of love.

So may my day be strong in Thee,
    Fed with the bread divine,
The sweet compassion of Thy life
    Be reproduced in mine.

So feed me, Lord, with spirit-food,
    So grant me strength from Thee,
That I may grow like to Thyself,
    Thine image, Lord, in me.

RALPH SPAULDING CUSHMAN

COMMUNION WITH GOD

"The communion of the body of Christ." The observance of the Lord's Supper does not make that communion. It is the form, among many others, in which the idea of that communion is most vividly enshrined. But in enshrining that idea, it enshrines another and a higher one—communion with God.

Through our daily communion with Christ, of which this supper is not the cause but the symbol, we realize, more deeply than we could do had He not been among us, our communion with God. We understand, through Christ's perfect communion with God, that we are right in claiming our communion with God. And that is the foremost need of man. To strive to dwell in God, and to feel Him dwelling in us, is at once the duty and the destiny of humanity.

STOPFORD A. BROOKE

DRINK YE ALL OF IT

" 'Drink ye all of it,' all, not just a sup—
   Drink my faith, my love," said Jesus,
"Drink the fullness of my cup.

" 'Drink ye all of it,' all, not just my peace—
   Drink my dangerous living, dying—
Drink my fearless, glad release.

" 'Drink ye all of it,' all, not just the sweet—
   Drink my bitter tears of anguish—
Drink the dregs of my defeat.

" 'Drink ye all of it,' all, not just my pain—
   Drink my joy of life abundant—
Drink my triumph, drink my reign!"

                E. DENT LACKEY

✧✧✧

PUT YOURSELF INTO THE PATH
OF THE WIND

"Where does the wind come from,
   Nicodemus?"
"Rabbi, I do not know;
Nor can you tell where it will go."

"Put yourself into the path of the wind,
   Nicodemus.
You will know the thrill of being borne
   along
By something greater than yourself.
You are proud of your position,
Of your security,
But you will perish in such stagnant air.

"Put yourself into the path of the wind,
   Nicodemus.
Bright leaves will dance before you.
You will find yourself in places
That you never dreamed of seeing.

You will be forced into places you have
   dreaded
And find them like a coming home.

"You will have a power that you never had
   before,
   Nicodemus.
You will be a new man!
Put yourself into the path of the wind."

                MYRA SCOVEL

✧✧✧

Remember the Guest we have within us.

                DOUGLAS V. STEERE

✧✧✧

Religion is God looking over your shoulder.

                REINHOLD NIEBUHR

✧✧✧

BENEATH THE FORMS OF
OUTWARD RITE

Beneath the forms of outward rite
   Thy supper, Lord, is spread
In every quiet upper room
   Where fainting souls are fed.

The bread is always consecrate
   Which men divide with men;
And every act of brotherhood
   Repeats Thy feast again.

The blessed cup is only passed
   True memory of Thee,
When life anew pours out its wine
   With rich sufficiency.

O Master, through these symbols shared,
   Thine own dear self impart,
That in our daily life may flame
   The passion of Thy heart.

                JAMES A. BLAISDELL

✥✥✥

COMMUNION

To take and then to give.
  To take His blood and then to give one's
    self,
Simply, as one would extend a gathered
    flower.
  To come because He calls, and because
    one would.
To make delight a duty.
  To feed on Him, not to offend His tender
    generosity,
And because there is no other bread that
    satisfies the soul.
  To link known past and unknown future
In one eternal present.
  To love and be loved by Him,
Until loving and being loved become one
    single act
  Alike of vital energy and rapt passivity.
To know that beauty is like He is.
  To see with the delicate non-vision of the
    blind.
To grasp the meaning of secrets hidden
  Not by darkness but by too much light.
To sense that worship is self-surrender,
  And to be human is to long for the
    Divine.
To realize that joy is what all life is made
    for,
  And that eternity will scarce be long
    enough.
To be untroubled by silence when words
    fail.
  To find, explore, delight in, rest upon,
The sweet and mighty Other,
  The everlasting Thou.

                    EDITH LOVEJOY PIERCE

✥✥✥

THE ANCIENT QUEST

Through all my years, in man and nature's
    face,

I've sought the Secret veiled behind the
    Scheme:
Why millions, fleeting as summer midges,
    teem,
And species sprout, and galaxies whirl in
    space.
Often, amid the dark, I've trailed a trace
Of light that beckoned and wavered like a
    dream,
Though high above, the Mystery arched su-
    preme—
The goal and guerdon of time's whirlpool
    race.

Yet through the fog, I've never lost a sense
Of some immortal, overmastering Aim
That sparks the grass, and fans the suns to
    flame.
And faith, while reason bows in impotence,
Still beams; and reasserts its earlier claim
Of some vast wisdom ruling life's Whither
    and Whence.

                    STANTON A. COBLENTZ

✥✥✥

A LOAF OF BREAD, A JUG OF WINE,
AND A TOWEL

The seed that's sown and harvested
  Becomes this blessed broken bread.

This blessed broken bread that's food
  For lasting peace and brotherhood.

The tree that's trained to yield this wine
  Will tell of sacrifice divine;

Of sacrifice My friends will make
  Before the Day of God will break.

My friends will never overlook
  What happened when this towel I took;

For all that bread and wine may say
  A towel will tell eternally.

                    JOHNSTONE G. PATRICK

Calvary

. . . in the Cross of Christ I glory

CROSS

❖❖❖

SCRIPTURE

I, if I be lifted up from the earth, will draw all men unto me.

JOHN 12:32

God forbid that I should glory, save in the cross of our Lord Jesus Christ, by whom the world is crucified unto me, and I unto the world.

GALATIANS 6:14

What things were gain to me, those I counted loss for Christ. Yea doubtless, and I count all things but loss for the excellency of the knowledge of Christ Jesus my Lord: for whom I have suffered the loss of all things . . . that I may win Christ, and be found in him, not having mine own righteousness, which is of the law, but that which is through the faith of Christ, the righteousness which is of God by faith: that I may know him, and the power of his resurrection, and the fellowship of his sufferings, being made conformable unto his death; if by any means I might attain unto the resurrection of the dead.

PHILIPPIANS 3:7–11

Rejoice, inasmuch as ye are partakers of Christ's sufferings; that, when his glory shall be revealed, ye may be glad also with exceeding joy.

I PETER 4:13

❖❖❖

MEDITATION

Golgotha, the place where Jesus was crucified, is better known in the Latin form as Calvary. The word "Calvary," meaning skull, refers either to the cranial shape of the spot or to its having been a place of execution. An ancient tradition says the Cross was raised above the place where Adam's skull had been buried. The Apostle Paul wrote, "For as in Adam all die, even so in Christ shall all be made alive."

Biblical and historical Christianity attribute many meanings to the death of Christ. The burden of both interpretation and ex-

perience is that the Cross is the source of our salvation and that in and through Christ's death reconciliation and a living relation with God are provided for the believer.

Jesus said, "Greater love hath no man than this, that a man lay down his life for his friends." When we read of the agony and sacrifice of Christ, so poignantly described in the Passion stories, we feel that He died not only for His friends who lived long ago but that He also died for each one of us.

The story of Jesus of Nazareth concerns One who, being the mightiest among the lowly and the lowliest among the mighty, has with His pierced hands turned the stream of history out of its course and lifted the gates of empires off their hinges.

JEAN PAUL RICHTER

❖❖❖

THE CROSS

When Christ went up the April roads
    The winds of April wept,
But through the woodway's early buds
    Triumphant murmur swept:
"On every height while time shall be
    Shall shine the glory of a Tree."

CHARLES L. O'DONNELL

❖❖❖

IN THE LIGHT OF THE CROSS

It has been the Cross which has revealed to good men that their goodness has not been good enough.

In its presence man dares not speculate about the degree of his goodness.

Rather he is at once cast down by his sin and overwhelmed by the joyous insight that God is the Kinsman of his way.

With Him alone he can produce a quality of living which will refashion the shambles of his world, stand it on its feet, shake the greed out of its pockets, brush off the grime of its hate and wash away the sullenness of its fear, so that it may become a fit dwelling place for the Kingdom of God.

JOHN C. SCHROEDER

❖❖❖

Calvary is an epitome of the world.

A. B. FAIRBAIRN

❖❖❖

JUSTICE AND MERCY

In the cross of Christ we glory, because we regard it as a matchless exhibition of the attributes of God.

We see there the love of God, desiring a way by which He might save mankind, aided by His wisdom, so that a plan is perfected by which the deed can be done without violation of truth and justice.

In the cross we see a strange conjunction of what once appeared to be two opposite qualities—justice and mercy.

We see how God is supremely just; as just as if He had no mercy, and yet infinitely merciful in the gift of His Son.

Mercy and justice, in fact, become counsel upon the same side, and irresistibly plead for the acquittal of the believing sinner.

We can never tell which of the attributes of God shines most glorious in the sacrifice of Christ; they each one find a glorious high throne in the person and work of the Lamb of God, that taketh away the sin of the world.

CHARLES H. SPURGEON

❖❖❖

TOWARD JERUSALEM

Opening our windows toward Jerusalem,
    And looking thitherward, we see
        First Bethlehem,
Then Nazareth and Galilee,
    And afterwards Gethsemane;
And then the little hill called Calvary.

AMY CARMICHAEL

❖❖❖

THE CENTER

The cross is central. It is struck into the middle of the world, into the middle of time, into the middle of destiny. The cross is struck into the heart of God.

FREDERICK W. NORWOOD

✦✦✦

HIS JERUSALEM AND OURS

Life holds for all the Jerusalem road, over which our unwilling feet must go. We cannot hope to match the heroic, selfless, dauntless spirit with which Jesus took that road. But we can, if we will, approximate it.

A disciple is not above his Master; but he can, if he so purposes, follow where the Master leads.

We cannot hope to escape the Jerusalems of life, nor should we deceive ourselves in the conceit that we can evade or escape the long, hard road without betraying the finer instincts of our souls.

EDGAR DE WITT JONES

✦✦✦

"PILATE WASHED HIS HANDS"

I washed my hands, but still I am distraught.
  I sense His shadow, haunting in appeal,
And there are moments when all Rome
    seems naught,
  So strong the urge to worship Him I feel.
I see His lash-marked back, His bloody
    brow;
  Again my fingers tremble in the bowl.
Like darts His silence cuts me, even now;
  Yet . . . Caesar's favor may appease my
    soul.

Nor did I dare to proffer Him my aid,
  When priests and elders, patriots I knew,
Cried for His death, advised me what to do
  With "that just Man" who was so un-
    afraid.
The thing is done! I washed my hands, and
    yet . . .
  His eyes upon me! How shall I forget?

IDA NORTON MUNSON

✦✦✦

TOWARD JERUSALEM

Yes, He must die! At length the end was
    writ
Beyond all lurking shadow of doubt in it.

And so, with steadfast eyes, He turned to go
    Toward Jerusalem.
Would we might know,
  Dear Christ, what deep new rapture of
    glory crowned
All the old wonder of the world around
  Thee, as Thou wentest, with unfaltering
    breath,
Along the inexorable road to death!
  Burst there ever such music from the
    bough
As the birds carolled, Lord, unto Thee
    now?
Blew there ever winds so fresh and free
Over the waters of Thy Galilee?
  Gleamed there ever such tender hints of
    grace
In even the most unholy human face?
  Or in Thine own ears rang before such
    sweet
Laughter of little children in the street?

Ah, this at last we know: the bluest skies
  Shine through the conquering spirit's
    agonies;
And ever the flowers bloom brightest unto
    them
  That set their faces toward Jerusalem.

GILBERT THOMAS

✦✦✦

THE GIFT

The cross was the gift of all Christ had. It was the seal of all He said. And it was the risk of all He hoped.

Somehow it stands for His fearless, gallant confidence in you and me.

It stands for His reckless adventure toward the Kingdom of God with nothing to rely on but the feet of men, and they fled; nothing but men's hands, and they nailed Him fast; nothing but men's hearts, and there weren't many that were even touched with pity!

That's the most astounding thing of all—that He knew how poor we are and still expected so richly of us.

PAUL SCHERER

165

✥✥✥

THIS SIDE OF CALVARY

We live on this side of Calvary. Had we lived on the other side of it, could we by any possible chance have expected to see the glory of the Resurrection, the transformation in the lives and outlook of the disciples, and the on-moving triumph of the great cause of Christ?

He wrote no books; He formed no great organization; His followers were, for the most part, "ignorant and unlearned men and women."

He exercised His ministry among a subject people of no particular political importance.

Falling foul of the authorities, He was condemned to a shameful death, and His followers were dispersed in terror lest a similar fate befall them.

Today the faith of Jesus is stronger than it has ever been. Millions throughout the centuries have loved Him and today thousands upon thousands are prepared to spend their lives in His service.

To ponder the story of the Cross and its amazing sequel is to be established in a faith that fosters great expectations and boundless hopes.

JOHN SHORT

✥✥✥

BARABBAS SPEAKS

I heard a man explaining
  (they said his name was Paul)
how Jesus, on that fateful day,
  had died to save us all.

I found it hard to follow
  His fine-spun theory,
but I am very, very sure
  He died that day for me.

EDWIN MCNEILL POTEAT

✥✥✥

All my life I have been seeking to climb out of the pit of my besetting sins. And I cannot do it. And I never will unless a hand is let down to draw me up.

SENECA

✥✥✥

ABOVE THE HILLS OF TIME

Above the hills of time the Cross is gleaming,
  Fair as the sun when night has turned to day;
And from it love's pure light is richly streaming,
  To cleanse the heart and banish sin away.
To this dear Cross the eyes of men are turning
  Today as in the ages lost to sight;
And for the love of Christ men's hearts are yearning
  As shipwrecked seamen yearn for morning light.

The Cross, O Christ, Thy wondrous love revealing,
  Awakes our hearts as with the light of morn,
And pardon o'er our sinful spirits stealing
  Tells us that we, in Thee, have been reborn.
Like echoes to sweet temple bells replying,
  Our hearts, O Lord, make answer to Thy love;
And we will love Thee with a love undying,
  Till we are gathered to Thy home above.

THOMAS TIPLADY

✥✥✥

The spirit of the cross must, as it were, be soaked into the very stuff and fiber of our mind. It must become the standard by which we judge everything, the background before which our whole life is enacted, so that that solemn shadow falls across it all and tells on every incident.

ARTHUR JOHN GOSSIP

RECOGNITION

When Christ went up to Calvary,
  His crown upon His head,
Each tree unto its fellow-tree
  In awful silence said:
"Behold the Gardener is He
  Of Eden and Gethsemane!"

JOHN BANISTER TABB

❖❖❖

UNDERSTANDING CALVARY

I feel that the great reason why we fail
to understand Calvary is not merely that
we are not profound enough; it is that
we are not good enough. It is because we
are such strangers to sacrifice that God's
sacrifice leaves us bewildered. It is because
we love so little that His love is mysterious.
We have never forgiven anybody at such
a cost as His. We have never taken the
initiative in putting a quarrel right with
His kind of unreserved willingness to suffer.
It is our unlikeness to God that hangs as
an obscuring screen impeding our view,
and we see the Atonement so often through
the frosted glass of our own lovelessness.

H. R. MACKINTOCH

❖❖❖

Like Judas,
we who are disciples
of the Master
may betray Him,
as Pilate could not.
Yet, if we betray Him,
it will resemble
the indifference of Pilate
more than the despair
of Judas.

MARION C. ALLEN

❖❖❖

FORGIVEN AND FORGIVING

We go to Calvary to learn how we may
be forgiven and to learn how to forgive
others, to intercede on their behalf, to join
the noble band of intercessors.

S. J. REID

❖❖❖

COSMIC SIGNIFICANCE

We see in the Cross what we have the
eyes to see.

The scribes and Pharisees saw in it the
end of a heretic.

The Romans saw in it the end of One
who trifles with the law.

The soldiers saw a fanatic who had stirred
up His fanatical people.

The disciples saw in it the loss of their
Friend and Master; some thought it pre-
mature and unnecessary; few if any understood what was happening.

Perhaps His mother alone knew that this
was more stupendous than any of them
realized.

It needed the thought of St. Paul, and
the long perspective of history, for men
to begin to understand something of what
had happened.

It is for us today just another good Man
sacrificing Himself for His cause; or it is
the most significant event on all the plane
of human history, an event with cosmic
significance for the relations between the
holy and living God, and sinful, guilty
humanity; and therefore with personal and
eternal significance for you and me.

SAMUEL M. SHOEMAKER

❖❖❖

Golgotha is dreadfully real: as real as suffering, as real as hard work and sacrifice, as
real as failure, as real as persecution.

VIRGIL A. KRAFT

STRENGTH

Ask of your soul this question, What is
    strength?
  Is it to slay ten thousand with the sword?
To steal at midnight Gaza's brazen gates?
  To raze a temple on a heathen horde?

Or, in a garden drenched with evening dew
  And bloody sweat, to pray beside a stone?
Defend a sinner from self-righteous priests?
  Bear up to Calvary a cross, alone?

JESSIE WILLMORE MURTON

GREAT UNEXPLORED WORLD

The death of Jesus has been the subject of
more thought, one can say without exagger-
ation, than anything that has occupied the
mind of man. No treatment of it ever satis-
fies listener or reader as complete or adequate; the best gives one the sense of having
touched, as it were, the mere hem of the
garment. Whenever we look at Him, and
think again of His death with any firmness
and reality, most of our previous thought
seems to be of little consequence, and we
are left with the feeling of a great un-
explored world before us, of more beyond.

T. R. GLOVER

DIALOGUE AT CALVARY

PROCULA: Do you think He is dead?
LONGINUS: No, lady, I don't.
PROCULA: Then where is He?
LONGINUS: Let loose in the world, lady,
  where neither Roman nor Jew can stop
  His truth.

JOHN MASEFIELD

WHY AND HOW THEY SUFFERED

Three crosses stood on Calvary's brow.
One man died there because He loved.
Two died because they hated. One hated
to the end. Another renounced hatred and
surrendered to love. The scene is a final
picture of the eternal opposition of love
and hatred. Love includes all the virtues;
hatred includes all the vices. The conflict
between Good and Evil ultimately nar-
rows to a titanic struggle between these
two forces.

Physical suffering was equally real for
the three men on Calvary's three crosses.
The difference lay in why they suffered
and how they suffered. Jesus was crucified
because He loved men, because He sought
to give life, because He dared resist evil.
The two thieves were crucified because
they hated men, because they sought to
take life, and because they dared resist
good. Hatred incarnated in them attempted to destroy love incarnated in
Jesus.

Thus, though the thieves shared the
suffering with Him, they also caused His
suffering. Evil kills both its friends and
its foes. It is death; it can never give
life. Good is life; it can never take life.
Hatred and love are the processes of life-
taking and life-giving.

TALMAGE C. JOHNSON

A THOUGHT

He who died on Calvary,
  Died to ransom you and me.

On the cross He bowed His head,
  In the grave He made His bed.

Ever since, the lilies bloom
  Round the portal of the tomb.

Ever since, o'er all our loss
  Shines the glory of the cross.

MARGARET E. SANGSTER

SIMON

Simon of Cyrene,
  Hear the frenzied feet
Of the maddened people
  Rushing down the street!

Hearken to their voices
  Sharper than the sword,
Like a breath of pestilence
  Cursing of the Lord!

Simon of Cyrene,
  Be thou stout of heart;
God has shed His grace on thee
  To do the noble part!

See, the good Lord cometh
  In a scarlet gown,
Bending to the burden
  Of His cross and crown!

Simon of Cyrene,
  Thou art glorified;
Jesus turned for help to thee
  And He was not denied!

EDGAR DANIEL KRAMER

❖❖❖

ALL HE COULD DO

The purpose of God in the history of man was accomplished when Jesus breathed His last upon the cross.

The cry "It is finished" was not the mere gasp of a wornout life; it was not the cry of satisfaction with which a career of pain and sorrow is terminated; it was the deliberate utterance of a clear consciousness on the part of God's appointed Revealer that now all has been done that could be done to make God known to men and to identify Him with men.

God's purpose had ever been one and indivisible—declared to men in various ways, a hint here, a broad light there, now by a gleam of insight in the mind of a prophet, now by a deed of heroism in king or leader, through rude symbolic contrivances and through the tenderest of human affections and the highest human thoughts. God had been making men ever more and more sensible that His one purpose was to come closer and closer into fellowship with them, and to draw them into a perfect harmony with Him.

Forgiveness and deliverance from sin were provided for them, knowledge of God's law and will, that they might learn to know and to serve Him—all these were secured when Jesus cried, "It is finished."

MARCUS DODS

❖❖❖

From THE FEET OF JUDAS

Christ washed the feet of Judas!
  The dark and evil passions of his soul,
His secret plot, and sordidness complete,
  His hate, his purposing, Christ knew the whole,
And still in love He stooped and washed His feet.

Christ washed the feet of Judas!
  Yet all his lurking sin was bare to Him,
His bargain with the priest, and more than this,
  In Olivet, beneath the moonlight dim,
Aforehand knew and felt his treacherous kiss.

Christ washed the feet of Judas!
  And thus a girded servant, self-abased,
Taught that no wrong this side of the gate of heaven
  Was ever too great to wholly be effaced,
And though unasked, in spirit be forgiven.

GEORGE MARION MC CLELLAND

❖❖❖

PRAYER ON GOOD FRIDAY

Blood of Jesus, shed for me,
  Cleanse my sin and make me free.

Let His life, so freely given,
  Heal our world asunder riven.

Let His words of love and peace
  Rule our lives till strife shall cease.

Let His faith, His grace and power,
  Be our strength in this dark hour.

Cross of Christ, undimmed by wrong,
  Be today my triumph song!

GEORGIA HARKNESS

❖❖❖

IN HOC SIGNO

The Kingdoms of the Earth go by
  In purple and in gold;
They rise, they triumph, and they die,
  And all their tale is told.

One Kingdom only is divine,
  One banner triumphs still;
Its King a servant, and its sign
  A gibbet on a hill.

GODFREY FOX BRADBY

❖❖❖

ONWARD AND UPWARD

I pass the vale. I breast the steep.
  I bear the cross: the cross bears me.
Light leads me on to light. I weep
  For joy at what I hope to see
When, scaled at last the arduous height,
  For every painful step I trod,
I traverse worlds on worlds of light,
  And pierce some deeper depth of God.

JOHN CHARLES EARLE

❖❖❖

CHRIST'S WAY

I read once a tale of how the Son of God, victorious over death, was ascending through the regions of heaven to His glorious Father, and, as He passed along one of the highest angels ventured to accost Him and to say, "My Lord, the great design, the inauguration of Thy Kingdom on the earth, is it all finished?"

And Jesus said, "It is finished!"

The angel said, "My Lord, I have been sent elsewhere, I have heard nothing: dare I ask what Thou hast done?"

Jesus replied: "I was known as the child of respectable working folk, I lived unnoticed for some thirty years, then I came forward for a few months and talked with men and women of all sorts, and I think some of those who listened will be influenced all their lives, some fishermen, some petty tradesmen, some women good and bad. And in the end enemies had me executed."

"My Lord, my Lord," exclaimed the angel in horror, "what, was there no other way?"

"No," said Jesus, "there was no other way."

F. C. BURKITT

❖❖❖

The Cross is God's seal and sign that He loves us and craves to forgive us in order to have us enter into the fellowship for which He created us.

The Cross is God's work in history whereby He has poked a hole in heaven's floor to let the divine light shine upon earth.

The Cross is the outlet from eternity into time of the power of God for salvation that comes with forgiveness.

Here God drilled through the partition between eternity and earthly time to admit the highest voltage wire of His love.

NELS F. S. FERRÉ

✤✤✤

FROM NAZARETH HE COMES

From Nazareth He comes, the Carpenter
    Who knows of hammering and blows
        that break
The worker's hands. From Galilee He
    comes,
    The Fisherman who walks upon the lake.

Through fields of harvest, ripe for pluck-
    ing grain;
    Along the dusty roads that go beside
The vineyards, Christ, the noble Carpen-
    ter,
    Goes to the city to be crucified.

Jerusalem's streets are filled with those
    Who cry, "Hosanna!" and others,
        "Crucify!"
For all of these He hangs upon the cross
    That lifts itself into the purple sky.

For all of these the Master lived and died.
    His lamp is tall and bright; our lamps
    are dim,
But we can see the way ahead of us,
    For where the Master goes we go with
    Him.

RAYMOND KRESENSKY

✤✤✤

THE FINAL TEST OF OUR
STEWARDSHIP

The only final test of our stewardship is
the Cross itself.

    The call to discipleship is the call to
die—the old self must die that the new
self may live.

    It is a strange paradox that with the
acceptance of the cost there comes the
unmistakable experience of joy.

    It is the joy of those who no longer
have to be perfect or have to succeed.

    It is the joy of those whose only purpose
is to do the will of God.

S. MACON COWLES

✤✤✤

SIMPLE FAITH

I am not wise
    Dear Lord, and yet
I ever dream
    Of Olivet.

Tomorrow is
    Dim mystery,
But I discern
    Gethsemane.

Though gray doubts leer,
    While tempests toss,
I lift mine eyes
    And see Thy cross.

Thine agony
    And bloody woe,
Dear Lord, is all
    I need—and know.

EDGAR DANIEL KRAMER

✤✤✤

JOSEPH OF ARIMATHAEA

Did Joseph have a feeling of regret:
    Perhaps some word unsaid—some deed
    undone,
That made him come in tenderness to get
    Christ's body from the cross? Yet he was
    one
Who was a counsellor, called good and
    just,
    And still the good and just can some-
    times fail . . .
He must have winced when thinking of
    the thrust
    Of thorny crown—flesh pierced by cruel
    nail.
I think he knelt with chastened, contrite
    heart,
    To wrap the body in its linen shroud,
And hoped this act would somehow heal
    the smart
    Of past neglect, and being thus allowed
The task, perhaps it helped him to
    atone—
    That he found peace beside that tomb
    of stone.

MARGARET E. BRUNER

172

Joseph's Garden

. . . the Lord is risen indeed

RESURRECTION

❖❖❖

SCRIPTURE

The first day of the week cometh Mary Magdalene early, when it was yet dark, unto the sepulchre, and seeth the stone taken away from the sepulchre. Then she runneth, and cometh to Simon Peter, and to the other disciple, whom Jesus loved, and saith unto them, They have taken away the Lord out of the sepulchre, and we know not where they have laid him. . . . Mary stood without at the sepulchre weeping: and as she wept, she stooped down, and looked into the sepulchre, and seeth two angels in white sitting, the one at the head, and the other at the feet, where the body of Jesus had lain. And they say unto her, Woman, why weepest thou? She saith unto them, Because they have taken away my Lord, and I know not where they have laid him. And when she had thus said, she turned herself back, and saw Jesus standing, and knew not that it was Jesus. Jesus saith unto her, Woman, why weepest thou? whom seekest thou? She, supposing him to be the gardener, saith unto him, Sir, if thou have borne him hence, tell me where thou hast laid him, and I will take him away. Jesus saith unto her, Mary. She turned herself, and saith unto him, Rabboni; which is to say, Master. Jesus saith unto her, Touch me not; for I am not yet ascended to my Father: but go to my brethren, and say unto them, I ascend unto my Father, and your Father; and to my God, and your God.

JOHN 20:1–2, 11–7

❖❖❖

MEDITATION

The Resurrection is the keystone of all Christian faith and history. It is the best-attested fact in the New Testament, where no fewer than ten appearances of the Risen Christ are recorded.

In the miracle of the empty tomb is found the power of God in its supreme manifestation.

This was the interpretation of the Resurrection in the early church. Paul wrote that Jesus was "declared to be the Son of God with power . . . by the resurrection from the dead."

The principalities and powers of this world were rendered impotent when Calvary's Victim walked victoriously from the garden of Joseph of Arimathaea.

Death had been conquered by life, hate had been overthrown by love, sin had been defeated through sacrifice. Men walked thenceforth in the newness of life, confident that as God had spoken the first word so also would the heavenly Father speak the final word.

The Resurrection was the joyous theme of apostolic preaching. The day of the Resurrection became ever after an occasion for prayer and praise. The door of the tomb became the radiant gateway to life and immortality.

Easter is the most spiritually energizing experience any man can know.

175

ECHOES OF JESUS

A little inn in Bethlehem first heard the
    echo of His voice,
    His footsteps on sands of Galilee
      aroused the ocean to rejoice,
And on the road to Calvary His gospel
    sounded near and far
    Like a reflected glory on the Cross of one
      great Star.

His gentle hands were joined with native
    wood cut from His native trees
    That echoed with the ax and hammer
      of His earthly enemies.
His body whispered sorrow in leaf of
    flesh, in branch of bone,
    But, oh, what strength sang from the soul
      that rolled away the stone!

                LUCILE COLEMAN

✦✦✦

REALITY

Not from two who supped with You
    At an inn as twilight fell
Do I know that Joseph's tomb
    Was an empty shell.

Not from Peter or from John
    Or from Mary or from Paul
Did I learn how life can change
    At Your call.

Not on the Damascus road
    Or in any far-off place
Did my spirit see the dawn
    On Your face.

Those who lived in Galilee
    Knew their Lord and held him dear—
But my Lord has come to me
    Now and here.

        AMELIA JOSEPHINE BURR

✦✦✦

CONTEMPORARY

To live in a world where Christ is risen
is to live in a world where Christ is our
contemporary: contemporary, not only in
the sense that He is never out of date,
but in the sense that He is here. We live
contemporaneously with Him.

                DANIEL T. NILES

✦✦✦

EASTER CONTRASTS

Out of the east comes new light after
the darkness of night. And we call it
morning. Out of the Easter morning came
a wondrous new light—the light of life—
after the darkness of sin's night. And it
has been the first gleam of a morning, the
morning of a new day, for all men.

Contrasts make things stand out. Black
touching white seems blacker, and white
looks whiter. Sorrow makes joy seem glad-
der. Joy makes sorrow seem sadder. The
deeper the sorrow, the greater is the uplift
of joy following, after the first daze is over.

That first Easter morning stood in
sharpest contrast with what went before.
The greatest possible contrast is between
life and death. All sorrow and darkness
and heaviness brood in the black world—
death. All gladness and brightness and
lightness gather up at their best in that
lightsome world—life.

                S. D. GORDON

✦✦✦

Easter heightens our appreciation of the
fact that reality is more than obvious.

It testifies that life is more than mere
duration.

It testifies that the soul is too big for
earth.

It assures us that death has been conquered.

                TEUNIS E. GOUWENS

✤✤✤

MARY MAGDALENE

At dawn she sought the Savior slain,
    To kiss the spot where He had lain
And weep warm tears, like springtime
    rain;

When lo, there stood, unstained of death,
    A Man that spoke with low sweet
    breath;
And "Master!" Mary answereth.

From out the far and fragrant years
    How sweeter than the songs of seers
That tender offering of tears!

RICHARD BURTON

✤✤✤

WHAT EASTER TELLS US

Easter tells us that the life awaiting us
beyond the grave is as certain as this life
that we are now living.

We do not need to speculate as to the
details of the life hereafter. It is where
Jesus Himself is, and that is enough.

Mary knew Jesus when she met Him in
the garden on the morning of the resurrection, and so we shall know our dear ones
when we meet them in the other life.

That life is not a vague and shadowy
and uncertain thing, but a life as real as
this one, in that sphere where Jesus now
is, where with those whom we have known
in this world we shall go on from strength
to strength in the life of perfect service,
in the heavenly Kingdom forever.

Easter tells us that Jesus Christ on the
throne of God is the one light and guide
for our life in this world and the one
hope for the world's future.

There is none other who can give us
the divine guidance that we need.

WILLIAM T. MANNING

✤✤✤

TRANSIENT

The biggest fact about Joseph's tomb was
that it wasn't a tomb at all. It was a room
for a transient. Jesus just stopped there
a night or two on His way back to glory.

HERBERT BOOTH SMITH

✤✤✤

FISHERS IN THE NIGHT

It was all over now. The populace
    Had slain the Master. Stoutly Peter
    swore,
"I go a-fishing." The two Zebedees
    Uncoiled the nets. They pushed off from
    the shore.
It was all over now: the dusty road,
    Beggars and Pharisees, the sick abed,
The sinners' hungry need, His face aflame,
    Two healing hands laid on an aching
    head.

It was all over now. The lake was cool.
    Vainly they labored through the night.
    The sun
Revealed the Master waiting on the sands.
    They beached to find that life was but
    begun.

BEULAH MAY

✤✤✤

The story of Easter is the story of God's
wonderful window of divine surprise.

CARL KNUDSEN

✤✤✤

ASSURANCE

It is not darkness you are going to, for
    God is light.
It is not lonely, for Christ is with you.
It is not an unknown country, for Christ
    is there.

CHARLES KINGSLEY

✤✤✤

PRAYER

O God, who in the resurrection of Jesus Christ hast assured us that love cannot be defeated by selfishness and hate, nor knowledge vanquished by ignorance, nor life holden of death, put new heart and hope and determination into us and all followers of Jesus to proclaim and stand for His Kingdom, in faith that all power in heaven and earth is confederate with him who obeys the Son of man.

Enable us to bring to the empty grave all our own purposes of good that have miscarried, our struggles for righteousness still unsuccessful, the disappointments which have made us doubt Thy love, and to confirm in Christ's triumph our confidence that however long the crucifixion may last, however securely buried may seem our aims of good, our plans of love, our trust and hope, the stone shall surely roll away, and all that is truly right and loving and Christlike prevail, through Him whom Thou hast made the Lord of life forever.

HENRY SLOANE COFFIN

From CHRISTMAS-EVE AND EASTER-DAY

Easter day breaks!
 Christ rises! Mercy every way is
  infinite—
Earth breaks up; time drops away;
 In flows heaven with its new day
Of endless life—
 What is left for us save in growth
Of soul to rise up . . .
 From the gift looking to the giver,
And from the cistern to the river,
 And from the finite to infinity,
And from man's dust to God's divinity.

ROBERT BROWNING

Eternal life is man's life when God has spoken His "yes" upon it, once for all, unconditionally and unreservedly, not to be changed any more.

Eternal life is man's life lived with God, in His bright life, nourished and sustained by His own life.

Eternal life is man's life committed to the service of God and thereby to the service of the neighbor, a life which certainly also serves him best who is allowed to live it.

Eternal life is man's indestructible life because it comes from God and is sustained by Him.

KARL BARTH

THE INNER RESURRECTION

Christ is ever rising again. Day by day men seek to bury Him under the debris of history, or embalm Him in creed and phrase and definition, or immure Him within the walls of churches and institutions, or smother Him under a load of the cares and riches and pleasures of this life, or stab Him to death with the daggers of their sins.

But always He rises, phoenixlike, from the ashes of the fires of selfishness and carelessness in which we allow His power over our lives to be destroyed.

Ever and again He is lifted up out of the common things of life, a vindication of His life and a triumph over the powers that did Him to death, and all men are drawn to Him as irresistibly as the earth is held in its orbit around the sun.

The empty tomb opens before the world, telling us it is God who still has the last word, not ourselves; that on Easter day life looks forward, onward, upward, God-ward.

ELMER S. FREEMAN

178

DEATH IS NOT DEATH

Death is not death if it kills no part of us, save that which hindered us from perfect life.

Death is not death, if it raises us in a moment from darkness into light, from weakness into strength, from sinfulness to holiness.

Death is not death, if it brings us nearer to Christ, who is the fount of life.

Death is not death, if it perfects our faith by sight, and lets us behold Him in whom we have believed.

Death is not death, if it gives us to those whom we have loved and lost, for whom we have lived, for whom we long to live again.

Death is not death, if it joins the child to the mother who is gone before.

Death is not death, if it takes away from that mother forever all a mother's anxieties, a mother's fears, and lets her see, in the gracious countenance of her Savior, a sure and certain pledge that those whom she has left behind are safe, safe with Christ and in Christ, through all the changes and dangers of this mortal life.

Death is not death, if it rids us of doubt and fear, of chance and change, of space and time, and all which space and time bring forth, and then destroy.

Death is not death; for Christ has conquered death, for Himself, and for those who trust in Him.

CHARLES KINGSLEY

❖❖❖

SOMETHING BEYOND

Every new experience with Christ tells us more about Heaven. In the days before the discovery of America, the Spanish coins carried a picture of the pillars of Hercules at the straits of Gibraltar and the inscription read "Ne plus ultra," meaning "There is nothing beyond." But after the courageous voyage of Columbus, the in-scription was altered to read "Plus ultra," meaning "Something beyond." Before the world knew Christ and His resurrection, the knowledge of Heaven was meager, but in His presence we are always saying "Plus ultra"—"Something beyond"—and that something we call Heaven.

A. PURNELL BAILEY

❖❖❖

CHRIST AND THE MOURNERS

Down on the shadowed stream of time and tears
  Voice of new grief and grief of ancient years—
Sad as when first from loving lips 'twas sighed—
  "Hadst Thou been here, my brother had not died."

Comfort us, Lord, who heard'st poor Martha's plaint,
  Heal the sore heart, uplift the spirit faint—
O Thou, the Peace that cometh after strife!
  O Thou, the Resurrection and the Life!

KATHERINE E. CONWAY

❖❖❖

We picture death as coming to destroy; let us rather picture Christ as coming to save.
We think of death as ending; let us rather think of life as beginning and that more abundantly.
We think of losing; let us think of gaining.
We think of parting; let us think of meeting.
We think of going away; let us think of arriving.
And as the voice of death whispers, "You must go from earth," let us hear the voice of Christ saying, "You are but coming to me!"

NORMAN MAC LEOD

MARY MAGDALENE

White the willow
   And white the thorn,
Where Mary walks
   This milk-white morn.

Leaves and petals
   Are still, so still,
And dew lies cold,
   So cold, so chill.

Sadly, slowly,
   She walks alone,
Thinking of One
   Behind a stone.

Walking, wishing,
   Eyes on the sod,
Hoping to hear
   The steps of God.

Would He could come,
   As once He came,
The Risen One
   Calling her name . . .

"Mary! Mary!" . . .
   Fast, oh faster . . .
Ah! speak Mary . . .
   "Master! Master!"

JOHNSTONE G. PATRICK

HIS DEATH AND RESURRECTION

In His death He is a sacrifice, satisfying
   for our sins;
In His resurrection, a conqueror;
In His ascension, a king;
In His intercession, a high priest.

MARTIN LUTHER

MIRACLES

On these electric branches
   The lightnings of the sun
Shall smite as Moses smote the rock
   And tides of life shall run.

The miracles of April
   God's first and fairest were.
The wonders of the earth are things
   Which constantly occur.

ROY HELTON

CHRIST IN THE BIBLE

He appears in Genesis as the Seed of the
   Woman.
   In Exodus, He is the Passover Lamb.
   In Leviticus, He is the Atoning Sacrifice.
   In Numbers, He is the Smitten Rock.
   In Deuteronomy, He is the Prophet.
   In Joshua, He is the Captain of the
      Lord's Hosts.
   In Judges, He is the Deliverer.
   In Ruth, He is the Heavenly Kinsman.
   In the six books of Kings, He is the
      Promised King.
   In Nehemiah, He is the Restorer of the
      nation.
   In Esther, He is the Advocate.
   In Job, He is my Redeemer.
   In Psalms, He is my All and in all.
   In Proverbs, He is my Pattern.
   In Ecclesiastes, He is my Goad.
   In the Song of Solomon, He is my
      Satisfier.
   In the Prophets, He is the coming
      Prince of Peace.
   In the Gospels, He is Christ coming to
      seek and to save.
   In Acts, He is Christ risen.
   In the Epistles, He is Christ at the
      Father's right hand.
   In the Revelation, He is Christ return-
      ing and reigning.

BILLY GRAHAM

CONVICTION

After Good Friday came Easter.

After the Cross came the Resurrection. Without the Resurrection the Cross would have spelled defeat, and the power of the Cross to change men's lives would not have been.

From the time of the earliest disciples the experience of men bears witness to the hope that came when His friends were convinced that the Cross was not the end, but that Jesus lived on, and in enhanced power, that the universe was so built that this life was not merely in His continuing influence but also in the enduring personal life of Jesus Himself.

The disciples were persuaded that Jesus lived, and that in His resurrection and His enriched life those who gave themselves to Him and followed Him would share in the eternal and growing life that was His.

They believed that because He lived they could live also.

Impelled by this conviction, the disciples went out to proclaim the good news to every creature.

From that experience and that conviction have come the transformed lives from every race and nation and clime and culture, the new movements which have sought to free man from the shackles of ignorance, slavery, disease, and despotism and to open to them what an early Christian called the "glorious liberty of the children of God."

KENNETH SCOTT LATOURETTE

❖❖❖

The story of the Christian is the story of many resurrections.

JOHN CALVIN

❖❖❖

I, TOO, HAVE KNOWN

I, too, have known Gethsemane
  In lonely tryst,
I have broken bread with Peter . . .
  By Judas kissed.

And grim frustrations I have known
  Of cherished plans,
Met Thomas-doubts instead of trust
  In many lands.

I, too, have known the rabble throng,
  Their taunts and jeers,
I, too, have borne the heavy cross
  'Mid scornful sneers.

But, oh, I've reached the heights sublime
  At dawn of day,
Known glorious triumphs when the stone
  Was rolled away.

MARGUERITE GEORGE

❖❖❖

HIS VICTORY

If ever anyone had a difficult conclusion to face, it was Jesus. Yet if He had given up in Gethsemane, unable to finish, all His teachings would have been forgotten, His works of mercy would have dropped into oblivion, and the life divine would have been wasted.

His victory lay in His power to say on Calvary, "It is finished."

If ever a man might have been tempted to give up it was Paul. Yet if in Nero's prison he had collapsed, unable to finish, all his fine start on the Damascus Road would have gone for nothing and his long arduous labor would have lost its fruit.

The significance of his life hung on his ability at last to say, "I have finished the course, I have kept the faith."

HARRY EMERSON FOSDICK

❖❖❖

APPROACHES

When thou turn'st away from ill,
  Christ is this side of thy hill.

When thou turnest toward good,
  Christ is walking in thy wood.

When thy heart says, "Father, pardon!"
  Then the Lord is in thy garden.

When stern Duty wakes to watch,
  Then His hand is on the latch.

But when Hope thy song doth rouse,
  Then the Lord is in the house.

When to love is all thy wit,
  Christ doth at thy table sit.

When God's will is thy heart's pole,
  Then is Christ thy very soul.

GEORGE MACDONALD

❖❖❖

NEW TESTAMENT APPEARANCES

These are the appearances referred to in the New Testament as having taken place between Easter morning and the Day of Ascension itself or the appearance to Paul.

They are as follows: (1) appearance to Mary Magdalene (Mark 16:9–11; John 20:11–18); (2) appearance to the company of women (Matt. 28:9–10); (3) appearance to Peter (Luke 24:34; 1 Cor. 15:5); (4) appearance to the two disciples, on the road to Emmaus (Mark 16:12–13; Luke 24:13–35); (5) appearance to the ten apostles in Jerusalem, Thomas being absent (Luke 24:36–43; John 20:19–23; since Mark speaks of eleven disciples, I would not include his reference here but in the sixth appearance; (6) appearance again to the apostles eight days later, Thomas being present (John 20:24–29 and possibly Mark 16:14); (7) appearance on the Sea of Galilee to the seven apostles (John 21); (8) appearance to the five hundred in Galilee (Matt. 28:16–20; 1 Cor. 15:6); (9) appearance to James (I Cor. 15:7).

This of course is not necessarily the order in which the appearances occurred. There could have been more than these. Indeed, from interpretation of Matt. 28:16 and 1 Cor. 15:6 I am inclined to believe Jesus met first with the eleven in Galilee, later with the five hundred. The appearance at the Ascension is given in Luke 24:50–51; Acts 1:6–9.

WILLIAM R. CANNON

❖❖❖

GOOD FRIDAY IN MY HEART

Good Friday in my heart! Fear and affright!
  My thoughts are the disciples when they fled,
My words the words that priest and soldier said,
  My deed the spear to desecrate the dead,
And day, Thy death therein, is changed to night.

Then Easter in my heart sends up the sun.
  My thoughts are Mary, when she turned to see,
My words are Peter, answering, "Lov'st thou me?"
  My deeds are all Thine own drawn close to Thee,
And night and day, since Thou dost rise, are one.

MARY ELIZABETH COLERIDGE

❖❖❖

A living Christ in a living man is a living sermon—the greatest sermon that can be preached.

ERNEST LLOYD

THE BRIDGE

There is a land of the living
and a land of the dead
and the bridge is love,
the only survival,
the only meaning.

THORTON WILDER
in THE BRIDGE OF SAN LUIS REY

From EASTER NIGHT

Public was Death; but Power, but Might,
But Life again, but Victory,
Were hushed within the dead of night,
The shutter'd dark, the secrecy.
And all alone, alone, alone,
He rose again behind the stone.

ALICE MEYNELL

The immortal Christ stands over against life and judges it by irradiating it. He sets the standard, shows what man is meant to be, revealing Himself in every demand on our generosity, and by that demand alone and our response to it separating the real from the unreal, the living from the dead.

EVELYN UNDERHILL

AN EASTER SONG

A song of sunshine through the rain,
    Of Spring across the snow;
A balm to heal the hurts of pain,
    A peace surpassing woe.
Lift up your heads, ye sorrowing ones,
    And be ye glad at heart,
For Calvary and Easter Day,
    Earth's saddest day and gladdest day,
Were just three days apart!

SUSAN COOLIDGE

GOD AND MAN

I am the harp
On which God plays,
Making music
In prayer and praise.

God is the wind,
And I the tree;
I bend the way
He blows on me.

God is the flame,
As tinder I
Catch fire each time
He passes by.

God is the bread
Of life and truth,
On Him I feed
My hungry youth.

Come, all the earth,
Come sit, come sup!
God is the wine
And I His cup.

JOHNSTONE G. PATRICK

EASTER BEATITUDES

Blessed are they of the Easter faith,
    For theirs is the risen Lord;
For them He lives, and to them He gives
    The fountain of life restored.

Blessed are they of the Easter cheer,
    For theirs is the burning heart;
For them the tomb is bereft of gloom,
    They walk with their Lord apart.

Blessed are they of the Easter hope,
    For theirs is the open gate;
It swings through the tomb to that other
    room
    Where the Lord and our loved ones
    wait.

CLARENCE M. BURKHOLDER

Mediterranean Sea

. . . go ye therefore and teach all nations

MISSIONS

❖❖❖

SCRIPTURE

I am the good shepherd, and know my sheep, and am known of mine. As the Father knoweth me, even so know I the Father: and I lay down my life for the sheep. And other sheep I have, which are not of this fold: them also I must bring, and they shall hear my voice; and there shall be one fold, and one shepherd.

JOHN 10:14–16

Go ye therefore, and teach all nations, baptizing them in the name of the Father, and of the Son, and of the Holy Ghost: teaching them to observe all things whatsoever I have commanded you: and, lo, I am with you alway, even unto the end of the world. Amen.

MATTHEW 28:19–20

As thou hast sent me into the world, even so have I also sent them into the world.

JOHN 17:18

Ye shall receive power, after that the Holy Ghost is come upon you: and ye shall be witnesses unto me both in Jerusalem, and in all Judaea, and in Samaria, and unto the uttermost part of the earth.

ACTS 1:8

❖❖❖

MEDITATION

The Great Commission at the close of Matthew's gospel represents Jesus' last word to His disciples and the first word in the vocabulary of all subsequent discipleship.

Into the mortal hands of the eleven remaining disciples Jesus placed His immortal tidings and into their hearts He implanted a world mission. They became His apostles, persons commissioned and sent as His representatives, empowered by His Spirit, and assured of His living presence.

Mission became the magnificent obsession of the early church and has been ever since the hallmark of radiant, venturesome, and consecrated Christian endeavor. Christianity is instinctively, incurably missionary.

The lamp lighted in Palestine was carried by Paul into Asia Minor and the Mediterranean world. Through the force of his skill, genius, and passion, "colonies of heaven" were established in the most strategic locations.

What must have seemed an impossible mission to the members of Christ's intimate circle of friends continues for us to be an incomplete mission until the witness and work of the Gospel embrace all humanity within the love, concern, and salvation of the benign Father.

187

WITNESS

A church is not new simply because a congregation was recently organized.

New churches are those—

that witness in depth to their congregations;

that dare to break the ties of tradition and to develop approaches and methods that meet the mood and temper of their communities;

that anticipate change and prepare for change;

that help their members recognize God's claim on their lives lest they stray and get lost in the wilderness of materialism and conformity that engulfs them;

that raise up within their ranks lay people who articulate their faith in daily life and work;

and that stay by their communities through all the changes that come.

THEODORE E. MATSON

❖❖❖

CHRIST'S SPIRIT

The Spirit of Christ is the spirit of missions, and the nearer we get to Him the more intensely missionary we must become.

HENRY MARTYN

❖❖❖

God called Peter from a fishing business, and Matthew from an office, and Livingstone from a loom, and Chalmers from a plough, and Moffat from a garden, and Mary Slessor from a mill, and they became immortal; but if the world is going to be filled with the glory of God, He must have His ministers in all these places, not only called from them.

LESLIE D. WEATHERHEAD

❖❖❖

PAUL

Bond-slave to Christ, and in my bonds
    rejoicing,
    Earmarked to Him I counted less than
      nought;
His man henceforward, eager to be voicing
    That wondrous Love which Saul the
      Roman sought.

Sought him and found him, working bitter
    sorrow;
    Found him and claimed him, chose him
      for His own;
Bound him in darkness, till the glorious
    morrow
    Unsealed his eyes to that he had not
      known.

JOHN OXENHAM

❖❖❖

IRRESISTIBLE TIDE

Fishermen, tax-gatherers, publicans and sinners, Samaritans, outcasts gathered about Him. From one to another the word was passed that here was a personality in whom one found the Life that was life indeed.

At His death this community became stronger rather than weaker. The heroic quality of life that was in the Founder became the possession of the group.

Like the irresistible tide that wave by wave encompasses the sand on the beach, so this movement took its triumphant course, proof against doubt, against argument, against opposition. Jewish councils could not successfully condemn its leaders, nor Roman prisons hold them.

Evangelists defied hardship and danger to make its messages known in every corner of the Empire. Death did not silence their message nor persecution weaken it.

This movement had about it a quality of life that was to overcome the world.

MARY ELY LYMAN

WHERE SHALL I WORK?

"Master, where shall I work today?"
    And my love flowed warm and free.
Then He pointed out a tiny plot
    And He said: "Work there for me."

But I answered quickly: "Oh, no, not
        there!
    Not any one could see,
No matter how well my task is done—
    Not that small place for me!"

And His voice, when He spoke, it was not
        stern,
    But He answered me tenderly:
"Disciple, search that heart of thine.
    Are you working for them, or for Me?
Nazareth was just a little place,
    And so was Galilee."

❖❖❖

PRAYER

O Thou who rulest by Thy providence over
land and sea, defend and guide and bless
the messengers of Christ; in danger be
their shield, in darkness be their hope;
enrich their word and work with wisdom,
joy and power, and let them gather souls
for Thee in far fields white unto the harvest.

O Thou who by Thy Holy Spirit work-
est wonders in secret, open the minds that
dimly look for light to see the day-star in
Christ; open the minds that seek the Unknown God to know their heavenly Father
in Christ; open the hearts that hunger for
righteousness to find eternal peace in
Christ. Deliver the poor prisoners of ignorance and captives of idolatry, break
down the bars of error, and dispel the
shadows of the ancient night; lift up the
gates, and let the King of Glory and the
Prince of Peace come in.

Thy Kingdom, O Christ, is an everlasting Kingdom! Strengthen Thy servants to
pray and labor and wait for its appearing;

forgive our little faith and the weakness of
our endeavor; hasten the day when all
nations shall be at peace with Thee, and
every land and every heart throughout the
world shall bless the name of the Lord
Jesus, to the glory of God the Father.

                        HENRY VAN DYKE

❖❖❖

WHOSO SUFFERS MOST

"I am the True Vine," said our Lord,
        "and ye,
    My brethren, are the branches," and
        that Vine,
Then first uplifted in its place, and hung
    With its first purple grapes, since then has
        grown,
Until its green leaves gladden half the
        world,
    And from its countless clusters rivers
        flow
For healing of the nations, and its boughs
    Innumerable stretch through all the
        earth,
Ever increasing, ever each entwined
    With each, all living from the Central
        Heart.
And you and I, my brethren, live and
        grow,
    Branches of that immortal human Stem.

Measure thy life by loss instead of gain;
    Not by the wine drunk, but the wine
        poured forth;
For love's strength standeth in love's
        sacrifice;
    And whoso suffers most hath most to
        give.

                    HARRIET ELEANOR KING

❖❖❖

YARDSTICK

The Christianity which is shared is the
Christianity which is convincing.

                    LYNN HAROLD HOUGH

❖❖❖

The romance and victory of the missionary enterprise is the story of living portraits of Jesus Christ.

EDGAR DE WITT JONES

❖❖❖

AFRICA

I slept. I dreamed. I seemed to climb a
  hard, ascending track
And just behind me labored one whose
  face was black.

I pitied him, but hour by hour he gained
  upon my path.
He stood beside me, stood upright, and
  then I turned in wrath.

"Go back," I cried, "what right have you
  to stand beside me here?"
I paused, struck dumb with fear, for lo!
  the black man was not there—

But Christ stood in his place!
And oh! the pain, the pain, the pain that
  looked from that dear face.

❖❖❖

SACRIFICE AND PRIVILEGE

People talk of the sacrifice I have made
in spending so much of my life in Africa.

Can that be called a sacrifice which is
simply paid back as a small part of a great
debt owing to our God, which we can
never repay?

Is that a sacrifice which brings its own
blest reward in healthful activity, the consciousness of doing good, peace of mind,
and a bright hope of a glorious destiny
hereafter?

Away with the word in such a view, and
with such a thought! It is emphatically no
sacrifice.

Say rather it is a privilege. Anxiety,
sickness, suffering, or danger, now and
then, with a forgoing of the common con-
veniences and charities of this life, may
make us pause, and cause the spirit to
waver, and the soul to sink; but let this
be only for a moment.

All these are nothing when compared
with the glory which shall hereafter be
revealed in, and for, us.

I never made a sacrifice.

Of this we ought not to talk, when we
remember the great sacrifice which He
made who left His Father's throne on high
to give Himself for us; "who being the
brightness of that Father's glory, and the
express image of His person, and uphold-
ing all things by the word of His power,
when He had by Himself purged our sins,
sat down on the right hand of the Majesty
on high."

DAVID LIVINGSTONE

❖❖❖

The moment we ourselves are saved, we
must set ourselves to saving others. The
way Christ became the Atoning Lamb was
by His hanging on the cross and dying
there. And Christianity for me means to
dedicate myself to serve others even unto
death. That, I am convinced, is the true
way of Jesus Christ. Christianity means to
save others. That is the way of the cross,
and the true way of Christ.

TOYOHIKO KAGAWA

❖❖❖

SEND ME

Use me, God, in Thy great harvest field,
  Which stretcheth far and wide like a
    wide sea;
The gatherers are so few; I fear the pre-
    cious yield
  Will suffer loss. Oh, find a place for me!
A place where best the strength I have will
    tell:
  It may be one the older toilers shun;
Be it a wide or narrow place, 'tis well
  So that the work it holds be only done.

CHRISTINA G. ROSSETTI

❖❖❖

OUR MISSIONARIES

Forget them not, O Christ, who stand
    Thy vanguard in the distant land!

In flood, in flame, in dark, in dread,
    Sustain, we pray, each lifted head!

Be Thou in every faithful breast,
    Be peace and happiness and rest!

Exalt them over every fear;
    In peril, come Thyself more near!

Let heaven above their pathway pour
    A radiance from its open door!

Turn Thou the hostile weapons, Lord,
    Rebuke each wrathful alien horde!

Thine are the loved for whom we crave
    That Thou wouldst keep them strong
      and brave.

Thine is the work they strive to do;
    Their foes so many, they so few.

Yet Thou art with them and Thy Name
    Forever lives, is aye the same.

Thy conquering Name, O Lord, we pray.
    Quench not its light in blood today!

Be with Thine own, the loved, who stand
    Christ's vanguard in the storm-swept
      land!

             MARGARET E. SANGSTER

❖❖❖

Life is a mission. Every other definition
is false and leads all who accept it astray.
Religion, science, philosophy, though still
at variance upon many points, all agree
in this, that every existence is an aim.

             GIUSEPPE MAZZINI

❖❖❖

From "BEHOLD, THE FIELDS ARE WHITE"

Where prophets' word, and martyrs' blood,
    And prayers of saints were sown,
We, to their labors entering in,
    Would reap where they have strown.

O Thou whose call our hearts has stirred!
    To do Thy will we come;
Thrust in our sickles at Thy word,
    And bear our harvest home.

             SAMUEL LONGFELLOW

❖❖❖

HEART BEATS

Home and foreign missions are alternate
beats of the same heart.

             E. STANLEY JONES

❖❖❖

INDEBTEDNESS

Very few of us would be Christians today
if there had not been missionaries yesterday.

             ROY L. SMITH

❖❖❖

Your love has a broken wing if it cannot
fly across the sea.

             MALTBIE D. BABCOCK

❖❖❖

WHEN THE DAYLIGHT WANES

No more in Galilee we look for Thee,
    O Risen Lord;
In every land and on each moonlit sea
    Thy voice is heard;
And when Thy saints are gathered in Thy
    name,
    Closer Thou art to each than fire to
    flame.

             THOMAS TIPLADY

Caesarea Philippi

. . . on this rock I will build my church

CHURCH

✦✦✦

SCRIPTURE

I was glad when they said unto me, Let us go into the house of the Lord.

PSALM 122:1

The Lord is in his holy temple: let all the earth keep silence before him.

HABAKKUK 2:20

Simon Peter answered and said, Thou art the Christ, the Son of the living God. And Jesus answered and said unto him, Blessed art thou, Simon Bar-jona: for flesh and blood hath not revealed it unto thee, but my Father which is in heaven. And I say also unto thee, That thou art Peter, and upon this rock I will build my church; and the gates of hell shall not prevail against it. And I will give unto thee the keys of the kingdom of heaven: and whatsoever thou shalt bind on earth shall be bound in heaven: and whatsoever thou shalt loose on earth shall be loosed in heaven.

MATTHEW 16:16–19

The Spirit of the Lord is upon me, because he hath anointed me to preach the gospel to the poor; he hath sent me to heal the broken-hearted, to preach deliverance to the captives, and recovering of sight to the blind, to set at liberty them that are bruised, to preach the acceptable year of the Lord.

LUKE 4:18–19

✦✦✦

MEDITATION

Fifty days after Easter and only ten days following the Ascension a remarkable experience transformed the small and loyal fellowship of Christ's disciples into a large and dynamic fellowship.

This dramatic occurrence, vividly recounted in Acts 2, resulted from the descent of the Holy Spirit and the consequent conversion of "about three thousand souls" from "every nation under heaven."

Known to us as Pentecost or Whitsunday—the latter because of the white clothing worn by persons seeking baptism on subsequent anniversaries of the Spirit's descent—marks the birthday of the Christian Church.

The Church, now a world-wide fellowship transcending all barriers of language, geography, and creed, is still empowered and sustained in worship and work by the Holy Spirit. The Spirit gives unity and fellowship to all men who acknowledge Christ as Lord and Savior.

❖❖❖

TRUE PENTECOST

The disciples received the Pentecostal power when they faced the Pentecostal task.

Pentecost began before they went to the upper room. It began when they ceased gazing upward into the skies on Mount Olivet and made their way back to Jerusalem.

In doing that they faced their world of need, of danger, of opportunity.

GEORGE C. PIDGEON

❖❖❖

HOUSE OF GOD

The Master looked out from Olivet toward the city. There was a wistfulness in His eyes that haunts my heart to this day, for He saw the past, the present, and the future.

What a story would those hills tell could they but speak! The tides of battle had swept about them like boisterous waves against a rock-strewn coast. David, the daring hero of Israel, had established his throne there, making Mount Zion his seat of power. Solomon, the splendid, had carried his father's schemes to completion, translating David's dreams into deeds.

The royal palace, the imposing towers and fortifications, were surpassed, however, by the House of God. The finest materials procurable had been fashioned by skilled craftsmen from afar. The project had laid hold of the popular imagination to a surprising extent. And when at last, after years of arduous toil, the work was finished, the Temple was consecrated to God amid a blaze of magnificence.

Then troubles came with the passing years. The city was besieged, the Temple ravaged and stripped by Nebuchadnezzar, and its rubble-strewn courts resounded with the desolate howl of jackals. Rebuilt by Zerubbabel, later desecrated by Antio-chus Epiphanes and reconsecrated by Judas Maccabaeus, yet like some grim warrior, its turbulent history was written in the scars deep graven on its frame. Then Herod the Great, an Edomite time-server, had razed it to the ground, and rebuilt it both as a salve to his conscience and a means of securing the support of Jewish patriotism for his throne.

There it stood, the visible symbol of Judah's invisible God, and about it the peaceful homes of the city. Why then the look of inexpressible anguish in the Savior's face? He saw what none other could see. The supersensitive soul has means of discerning the truth which others miss.

J. W. G. WARD

❖❖❖

Christendom has never been divided in the chambers where good men pray.

WILLIAM RALPH INGE

❖❖❖

VIA LUCIS

And have the bright immensities
   Received our risen Lord
Where light-years frame the Pleiades
   And point Orion's sword?

Do flaming suns His footsteps trace
   Through corridors sublime,
The Lord of interstellar space
   And Conqueror of time?

The heaven that hides Him from our sight
   Knows neither near nor far:
An altar candle sheds its light
   As surely as a star;

And where His loving people meet
   To share the gift divine,
There stands He with unhurrying feet,
   There heavenly splendors shine.

HOWARD CHANDLER ROBBINS

❖❖❖

CORPORATE WORSHIP

There is nothing more illuminating, more ennobling, than to be one of a company of people who have come together in order to free their spirit from entangling personal bonds, quiet their soul by silence, release their aspiration by music and poetry, concentrate their mind on spoken wisdom, open their heart to all that is good, true, and beautiful, thus to tune themselves to God and to come into touch with Jesus Christ.

MURIEL LESTER

❖❖❖

A COUNTRY CHURCH

I think God seeks this house, serenely
    white,
    Upon this hushed, elm-bordered street,
    as one
With many mansions seeks, in calm delight,
    A boyhood cottage intimate with sun.

I think God feels Himself the Owner
    here,
    Not just rich Host to some self-seeking
    throng,
But Friend of village folk who want Him
    near
    And offer Him simplicity and song.

No stained-glass windows hide the world
    from view,
    And it is well. The world is lovely
    there,
Beyond clear panes, where branch-scrolled
    skies look through,
    And fields and hills, in morning hours
    of prayer.

God spent His youth with field and hill
    and tree,
    And Christ grew up in rural Galilee.

VIOLET ALLEYN STOREY

❖❖❖

Had we been on the mountainside of Capernaum some twenty centuries ago, mingled with the shepherd and fisherman audience of Galilee;

had we felt the upland breath of that autumn evening on whose wings the great Teacher's accents rose and died away;

had we marked the eyes of Jesus, invited by the note of a bird whirling overhead or caught by the beauty of a distant lily floating in the Lake of Galilee or as He pointed to the pastures brilliant with gold amaryllis and heard His praise of the flowers that toil not;

had we seen Him point to the green grass which carpets the mountainside and heard Him draw from all other beauties of nature lessons that Heaven tells—

we should have been ashamed of our want of trust in Him who made us.

FULTON J. SHEEN

❖❖❖

HYMN

Wider grows the kingdom,
    Reign of love and light;
For it we must labor,
    Till our faith is sight.

Prophets have proclaimed it,
    Martyrs testified,
Poets sung its glory,
    Heroes for it died.

Forward through the ages,
    In unbroken line,
Move the faithful spirits
    At the call divine.

FREDERICK L. HOSMER

❖❖❖

Down over the hills of the centuries marches a slender line of sincere Christians. That line has always been thin, but always the cross has gone on before and the influence has been beyond measure.

WILLIAM RALPH INGE

THE GREAT NAME IN HISTORY

Jesus Christ is the great name in history. There are others for whom men have died; He alone is adored by all people, in all nations, and in all times.

He who bears this name is known throughout the world. Even among the savage and degenerate tribes of the human race, His apostles preach without ceasing that He died upon the Cross; and the off-scourings of mankind may be saved by loving Him. Those who are neutral, in the modern world, recognize that none is better for the weak and miserable.

The greatest intellects of the past would be forgotten if memorials, as palaces, obelisks or tombs, if written testimonies, as papyrus or parchments, bricks, columns, or medals, had not preserved their memory. Jesus survives in the conscience of the faithful. There is His witness and indestructible monument. The church founded by Him fills time and space with His name. She knows Him, she loves Him, she adores Him.

HENRI DIDON

❖❖❖

The people who love Christ are not apart. Like the soft, glorious Pleiades they keep together in the sky.

STORM JAMESON

❖❖❖

HOLY MOMENT

The holiest moment of the church service is the moment when God's people—strengthened by preaching and sacrament —go out of the church door into the world *to be the Church.* We do not go to church; we are the Church.

ERNEST SOUTHCOTT

❖❖❖

PETITION

Be, Lord, within me to strengthen me,
without me to guard me,
over me to shelter me,
beneath me to establish me,
before me to guide me,
after me to forward me,
round me to secure me.

LANCELOT ANDREWES

❖❖❖

The soul communing with God, a heart drenched with a dream, a life lured by love—where these are, there is Pentecost.

WILLIAM H. BODDY

❖❖❖

DIVINE ECONOMY

My greatest loss: to lose my soul.

My greatest gain: Christ my Savior.

My greatest object: to glorify God.

My greatest pride: a crown of glory.

My greatest work: to win souls for Christ.

My greatest joy: the joy of God's salvation.

My greatest inheritance: heaven and its glories.

My greatest victory: victory over death through Christ.

My greatest neglect: to neglect so great a salvation.

My greatest crime: to reject Christ, the only Savior.

My greatest privilege: power to become a son of God.

My greatest bargain: the loss of all things to win Christ.

My greatest profit: godliness in this life and that to come.

My greatest peace: the peace that passeth understanding.

My greatest knowledge: to know God and Jesus Christ whom He hath sent.

J. E. DINGER

❖❖❖

WHAT IS THE CHURCH?

What is the church? What is its very essence and mission? The church is a living social and spiritual organism through which flows the life of the great Master Spirit of humanity, Jesus Christ. Each individual church is a branch of this Living Vine. The church as a whole is the continuation of the Christ personality —His spirit and ideals. It is His living representative, His organ of expression, His continual reincarnation. This gives to the church a unique character and mission, and one that involves much sacrificial devotion.

JOHN WRIGHT BUCKHAM

❖❖❖

SAVIOR TRIUMPHANT

What a folly would it be to suppose that Christ, after having finished His great work, overcame death, ascended into heaven, with all power in heaven and on earth, was become less a Savior and gave less certain and immediate help to those that by faith turn to Him now, than when He was clothed with the infirmity of our flesh and blood upon earth.

Has He less power after He has conquered than whilst He was only resisting and fighting with our enemies?

Or has He less good will to assist His church, His own body, now He is in heaven, than He had to assist publicans and sinners before He was glorified as the Redeemer of the world?

WILLIAM LAW

❖❖❖

Sunday we give to joy.

TERTULLIAN

❖❖❖

A saint is simply a human being whose soul has grown up to its full stature by

full and generous response to its environment—God.

EVELYN UNDERHILL

❖❖❖

MAKING OUR ANCESTORS OUR CONTEMPORARIES

The Christian tradition comes to us most potently as the gift of twenty centuries of dead men. For Christianity includes all that it has done for men during the last two thousand years.

It includes all that men have become through the influence of Jesus Christ. It includes all that men have done under His inspiration.

You cannot deprive the Apostle Paul of the right to vote at any Christian convocation because he is dead.

And Boniface from the German forests, and the monk Augustine in early England, and Patrick in Ireland, and Carey in India, and Livingstone in Africa belong to every Christian assembly.

And Origen from Alexandria, and Chrysostom from Constantinople, and the great Bishop of Hippo from Africa, and Anselm from eleventh-century England, and Saint Francis from thirteenth-century Italy come to do commerce with us today.

It takes everything that has ever happened to all the saints and martyrs and thinkers and men of action inspired by Christ to make up the Christian Church.

From every Christian century they come hurrying to councils vaster and more potent than Nicaea. And as we allow them all to speak, and as we allow them all to vote, we begin really to understand the quality and the meaning of the Christian religion.

It is only when all our Christian ancestors are allowed to become our contemporaries that the real splendor of the Christian faith and the Christian life begins to dawn upon us.

LYNN HAROLD HOUGH

PENTECOST OF LOVE

If the old hurt and heartache of the world is to be healed, if there is to be love where now there is hate; if bitter racial rancors are to be cleansed away, if the shadow of war is to be lifted from the life of man, setting us free to create a world fellowship; if the race is to be led toward a juster, wiser, more merciful social order, and the light of the gospel sent into all the dark corners of the earth; it will be by the union of those who have found in Jesus the way, the truth, and the life—by a pentecost of love and a baptism of brotherhood. Nothing can save the Church and make it equal to the tragic necessities of our age except the power of Him who created it—nothing but the red passion of the love of God and the white fire of His Spirit in our hearts.

JOSEPH FORT NEWTON

❖❖❖

JESUS WROTE WITH HIS FINGER ON THE GROUND

Writing is made on stone, on leather, and
    on clay,
On paper spread afar to last for many a
    day.
Only the Word of God come down from
    heaven dare trust
His writing to the dust
That shall be swept away.

Writing is made by steel, by chisel, or
    by pen,
Or printed blackly down again and yet
    again.
Only the Word of God can be so very
    sure
His writing will endure,
Traced lightly by His finger on the hearts
    of men.

EDITH LOVEJOY PIERCE

Worship is the disciplined opening of the self to God.

GREGORY VLASTOS

❖❖❖

ARTIST

Christ was more of an artist than all the others. He worked in living flesh.

VINCENT VAN GOGH

❖❖❖

He is an apostle only as whatever capacities he possesses are wholly open to use for the purposes of God.

DOUGLAS V. STEERE

❖❖❖

LIVING SAVIOR

No wonder if the Christians made an impression out of all proportion to their numbers. Conviction in the midst of waverers, fiery energy in a world of disillusion, purity in an age of easy morals, firm brotherhood in a loose society, heroic courage in time of persecution, formed a problem that could not be set aside, however polite society might affect to ignore it: and the religion of the future turned on the answer to it. Would the world be able to explain it better than the Christians, who said it was the living power of the risen Savior?

H. M. GWATKIN

❖❖❖

WITNESS

There is much that is wrong with our Christian witness, but the thing that is most wrong is the absence of joy.

WILLIAM C. NELSON

❖❖❖

PRAYER

By Thy entry into Jerusalem,
Give us courage to accept the issues of
    our faith.

By Thy cleansing of the Temple,
Give us zeal for righteousness and for Thy
    holy church.

By the breaking of bread and giving of
    the cup,
Help us to give ourselves for the life of
    the world.

By Thy washing of the disciples' feet,
Take away our pride and endue us with
    Thy spirit of true humility.

By Thy acceptance in the garden of the
    will of God,
Help us to seek to learn the will of God
    and to surrender our own will to it.

By Thy forgiveness of those who nailed
    Thee to the cross,
Make us ready to forgive.

By Thy faithfulness unto death, even the
    death of the cross,
Make us steadfast in our faith to our
    life's end.

PRAYER FOR ALL OCCASIONS

❖❖❖

MARY AT THE WELL

I fill my jar
    With drops that hold the colors of a star.
If I must walk at last, some darker way,
    My heart shall hold this one immortal
        day,
And a Child's loveliness at play.
    With seven sunbeams in His hair, my
        Jesus stands,
Pouring the drops like broken jewels
    through His hands.

With twenty sunbeams in His heart of
    gold,
He gives me little precious words to hold:
    "When I am taller grown than all the
        sons of men,
I shall bring water so you do not thirst
    again—
    Cold drops of crystal from a stream
Hidden in some white dream."

My heart within me is a cage of singing
    birds,
    Keeping His lovely words.
His very thoughts are flower buds, tightly
    curled,
    Until their day of blossoming through
        the world.
A little happier than other women are,
    I bend as they, to fill my earthen jar,
With drops that hold the mysteries of a
    star.

MARY BRENT WHITESIDE

❖❖❖

AS SOMETIMES, IN A TALE

As sometimes, in an intricate tale, we find
No outlet from the plot's fast-darkening
    maze,
Yet finally, through the straits of struggle,
    wind
To clear blue summits in a sunny blaze—

So too, in life, when all seems meshed and
    coiled,
The Master of the Story may create,
Out of the web wherein we bitterly toiled,
A pathway to the shining, longed-for gate.

STANTON A. COBLENTZ

❖❖❖

ENTRANCE

When I go into the Light,
I will take my neighbor
with me into that Light.

ST. CATHERINE OF SIENA

202

A PRAYER POEM

O Master of the loving heart,
  The Friend of all in need,
We pray that we may be like Thee
  In thought and word and deed.

Thy days were full of kindly acts;
  Thy speech was true and plain;
And no one ever sought Thee, Lord,
  Or came to Thee in vain.

Thy hand was warm with sympathy;
  Thy hand God's strength revealed;
Who saw Thy face or felt Thy touch
  Were comforted and healed.

O grant us hearts like Thine, dear Lord;
  So joyous, true and free
That all Thy children everywhere
  Be drawn by us to Thee.

CALVIN W. LAUFER

❖❖❖

THE CHURCH OF OUR LORD

What makes a church great?
Not soft seats and a subdued light
  . . . but strong courageous leadership.
Not the sweet tones of the organ
  . . . but sweet personalities that some-
    how reflect Jesus.
Not the tall towers with chimes and bells
  . . . but the lofty vision of its people.
Not the finances received
  . . . but the services rendered.
Not a large membership
  . . . but God's presence and direction
    and power.
Not what has been done in the past
  . . . but what is being done today and
    will be done tomorrow.

BAPTIST HERALD

❖❖❖

ALTARS

A man I know has made an altar of his factory bench. And one has turned the counter of his store into a place of sacrifice and holy ministry.

Another still has changed his office desk into a pulpit desk from which to speak and write, transforming commonplace affairs into the business of the King.

A Martha in our midst has made her kitchen table a communion table.

A postman makes his daily rounds a walk in the temple of God.

To all these each daily happening has come to be a whisper from the lips of God, each separate task a listening post, each common circumstance a wayside shrine.

EDGAR FRANK

❖❖❖

NOTHING NEW

The Master came two thousand years ago,
Into a troubled world of selfishness,
And when He saw man's hatred here
  below,
He went among the crowds to pray and
  bless.
Within the silence of the hills He trod
To meditate upon the ways of men,
And then He gave them lessons fresh
  from God,
And taught them love and healed their
  sick again.

With simple parables, great truth He gave—
That as they sowed, so also should they
  reap,
That love could never fail—that love would
  save,
That love was the commandment they
  must keep.
And there is nothing new that men should
  know—
Just lessons taught two thousand years ago.

BETTY L. WHITSELL

WITNESS

Not merely in the words you say,
   Not only in your deeds confessed,
But in the most unconscious way
   Is Christ expressed.

Is it a beatific smile?
   A holy light upon your brow?
Oh, no; I felt His presence while
   You laughed just now.

For me 'twas not the truth you taught,
   To you so clear, to me still dim,
But when you came you brought
   A sense of Him.

And from your eyes He beckons me,
   And from your heart His love is shed,
Till I lose sight of you, and see
   The Christ instead.

❖❖❖

In my brother, Christ offers me Himself
to be loved.

HARLAND G. LEWIS

❖❖❖

INSCRIPTION

God, make the door of this house we have
   raised to Thee
Wide enough to receive all who need
   human love and fellowship and a Father's
   care,
And narrow enough to shut out all envy,
   pride, and hate.
God, make the door of this house the
   gateway to Thy eternal Kingdom.

❖❖❖

Believing in Christ as Savior is inseparable
from being a Christian to your neighbor.

MARTIN LUTHER

❖❖❖

Love penetrates to the possibilities.

GEORGE SANTAYANA

❖❖❖

WORSHIP

I magnify Thee, Lord, to see Thy light:
As the big mirror on Mount Palomar
Focuses beams from a distant star,
Bringing the invisible into sight,
So does my worship help me see Thy might
And grace. Not that Thou art so faint or
   far,
But that my eye is dim, my senses dull,
My thoughts distracted and my heart too
   full
Of secondary things. The earth and air
Are full of Thy glory—yet I fail to see
Until I stop and yield myself in prayer;
Then does Thy sovereignty dawn over me.
Hallowed be Thy name! Let me be still
And make my choice the serving of Thy
   will.

HUGH STEVENSON TIGNER

❖❖❖

ON THE APOSTLES' CREED

We live our fragmentary lives and sink in
fragmentary thoughts. We seldom see reality as whole, a unity.

We smile on birth as part of life, yet
shrink from contemplating death; we see
no link between the two. That there may
somehow be a meaning which runs
through nativity and growth and pain and
death we can't forethink.

It therefore lends us comprehensiveness
to see that our belief in God's design swells
from creation to the present day; and that
conception, birth, and living, yes, and
death and resurrection, mark a line of
march for all who follow Him, the Way.

TERENCE Y. MULLINS

Palestine

. . . consider the lilies of the field

BEAUTY

❖❖❖

SCRIPTURE

I will lift up mine eyes unto the hills, from whence cometh my help.
My help cometh from the Lord, which made heaven and earth.

PSALM 121:1–2

Blessed of the Lord be his land, for the precious things of heaven, for
the dew, and for the deep that coucheth beneath, and for the
precious fruits brought forth by the sun, and for the precious things
put forth by the moon, and for the chief things of the ancient
mountains, and for the precious things of the lasting hills, and for
the precious things of the earth and the fulness thereof.

DEUTERONOMY 33:13–16

Consider the lilies of the field, how they grow; they toil not, neither
do they spin: and yet I say unto you, That even Solomon in all his
glory was not arrayed like one of these.

MATTHEW 6:28–29

❖❖❖

MEDITATION

Palestine is the spiritual home of the Christian's heart and in a sense the place where his soul finds a natural and congenial residence.

Even Christians who have not made pilgrimages to those places forever hallowed by the footsteps and words of the Master can identify by name and location hills and lakes and villages. Each time we open our Bible some aspect of this land and people is imprinted in our memory. Always in our minds we see Christ at a familiar well, at the shoreline, or ascending to a mountain's crest in this land God chose and preserved for patriarch, priest, and prophet.

The Hebrew people tenaciously clung to their land and were responsive to the beauty, majesty, and orderliness of their natural surroundings. God spoke to them in wind and wave, in storm and quiet nightfall. "The heavens declare the glory of God; and the firmament sheweth his handiwork. Day unto day uttereth speech, and night unto night sheweth knowledge."

Biblical Palestine, whose borders changed according to the vexations of history, was relatively small, the distance "from Dan to Beer-sheba" being little more than 150 miles and encompassing no more than 10,000 square miles.

Great variation in soil, rainfall, temperature, and elevation made it a land of considerable diversity. But to our spiritual fathers it was supremely "a good land" and "a land flowing with milk and honey."

✦✦✦

JESUS WAS A POET

Jesus was a poet—
　He spoke in singing words
Of gold wheat and its sowing,
　Of little feathered birds;
He told of one repentant
　Who had set himself to roam,
And many a pilgrim, harking,
　Has wept and turned toward home.

He sang of vine and fig tree,
　Of water and of bread,
Of sheep and a good shepherd,
　And every word He said
Is pregnant with deep meaning
　To pierce the listener through·
Strong words that live forever
　As great poetry should do.
And though no single stanza
　Has balanced form or rhyme,
Yet Jesus is the greatest
　Poet of all time.

GRACE NOLL CROWELL

✦✦✦

ACTS OF BEAUTY

The completed beauty of Christ's life is only the added beauty of little inconspicuous acts of beauty—
　talking with the woman at the well;
　going far up into the North country to talk with the Syrophenician woman;
　showing the young ruler the stealthy ambition laid away in his heart that kept him out of the kingdom of Heaven;
　shedding a tear at the grave of Lazarus;
　teaching a little knot of followers how to pray;
　preaching the Gospel one Sunday afternoon to two disciples going out to Emmaus;
　kindling a fire and broiling fish that His disciples might have a breakfast waiting for them when they came ashore from a night of fishing, cold, tired, and discouraged.

CHARLES HENRY PARKHURST

✦✦✦

INSPIRED TO PRAISE

To the Biblical man, the beauty of the world issued from the grandeur of God; His majesty towered beyond the breathtaking mystery of the universe. Rather than being crushed by the mystery, he was inspired to praise the majesty. And rather than praise the world for its beauty, he called the world to praise its Creator.

ABRAHAM J. HESCHEL

✦✦✦

THE LILIES OF THE FIELD

When I went up to Nazareth—
　A pilgrim of the spring—
When I went up to Nazareth
　The earth was blossoming!
I saw the blue flower of the flax
　Beside a shepherd's fold;
Along the hillsides' stony tracks
　I found the marigold;
The iris raised a shimmering spire
　Of beauty at my feet;
The poppy was a cup of fire
　Among the cooling wheat!

When I went up to Nazareth
　I marked how time came down
With blighting dust and withering breath
　Upon the hallowed town!
The years that buried Babylon
　Were drifting to efface
The steps of Mary's Heavenly Son,
　But still His truth held place,
And still I read His permanence
　By signs that never dim:
With all their ancient eloquence;
　The lilies spoke of Him

DANIEL HENDERSON

✦✦✦

A SERMON OF THE SKY

When the Hebrew came and walked out among the starry constellations, he saw it was God that has brought the glory down and let it be, and let the noon light shine on him with its glorious torch.

He could not let the solar luster be unhuman. He could not let the glory fall in his eyes and ask no amazing, passionate question. But, instead, when he saw glory, he saw through it the heavenly face as through an open window, and saw Him—Him!

And the heavens, to the Hebrew mind, declared the glory of God. That is why the Hebrew vocabulary and understanding and poesy and profundity answer to the human heart.

And this race of people, this nation, as it was the nation of thousands of years ago, was never content to let things rest as things.

Behind the mathematics they sought the mathematician; behind the door they sought the maker of the door, and behind the stairway they sought the carpenter who built the stair, and behind the constellations they looked for the fingers of fire that flung the stars out into space.

WILLIAM A. QUAYLE

❖❖❖

APOCALYPSE

I ask for heaven no brighter blue than this,
    No street more golden that this quiet
        lane—
The bending, sun-flecked branches stoop
        to kiss
    The shadowy bank, where lately summer
        rain
Has come to garnish thus the common sod
    And make each blade of grass a glitter-
        ing gem.
Lo! here I see the temple of our God,
    The holy city of Jerusalem.

RUTH FROST

❖❖❖

HE, TOO, LOVED BEAUTY

I who love beauty in the open valleys,
    Tintings of sunset, and the swallow's
        flight,
Must breathe the air of squalid city alleys,
    Shut from the cool caresses of the night.
Wistful of fragrance where the springtime
        dallies,
    Sharing with sordid souls a city's blight.

He, too, loved beauty, but a city drew
        Him.
    Flowers He found in little children's
        eyes;
Something of grace in lepers stumbling
        to Him;
    Fragrance of spikenard spilt in sweet
        surprise;
Joy in forgiving men at last who slew Him;
    Courage in service, hope in sacrifice.

EDWIN MC NEILL POTEAT

❖❖❖

PERPETUAL MIRACLE

Go out into a garden and examine a seed; examine the same plant in the bud and in the fruit, and you must confess the whole process is a miracle, a perpetual miracle. Take it at any period, make yourself as familiar with all the facts as you can at each period, and in each explanation there will be some step or appearance to be referred directly to the Great Creator; something not the effect of the sower's deposit, nor of the waterer's hope. It is not the loam, nor the gravel, it is not the furrow of the ploughshare, nor the glare of the sun that calls greenness from the dust, it is the present power of Him who said, "Seed-time and harvest shall not fail." Needs there, my brethren, any other book than this returning summer that reminds us of the first creation, to suggest the Presence of God?

RALPH WALDO EMERSON

THE MIGHTY POEM

That God is a spirit has not hindered Him from shaping the vault of night and hanging it with stars;

from tinting the tender blue of day, save where it shrinks from the golden glory of the sun;

from spreading the sheet of sea and streaking it with green and gold;

from poising the summer clouds to fling the chase of purple shadows on the hills;

from shining through the cool light of the spring woods;

from dwelling in our humanity to touch it with many a grace and repeat in it the image of His pity and His truth;

from resting with the Man of Sorrows as the symbol of His divine purity and holy love.

These are the works of His creativeness, the appeal of His beauty to our hearts, the mighty poem He improvises through all the rhythm of the universe.

JAMES MARTINEAU

❖❖❖

A PRAYER

Each day I walk with wonder
  'Neath skies or dark or fair;
Over, around, and under
  Are marvels that I share.

Whate'er the bonds of duty,
  The gyves that grip and thrall,
The luring call of beauty
  Is greater than them all.

I pray I may be shriven
  Should I fail more or less,—
That I may be forgiven
  For following loveliness!

CLINTON SCOLLARD

❖❖❖

CONVERSATION

Christ talked of grass, and wind, and rain,
  And fig-trees and fair weather,
And made it His delight to bring
  Heaven and the earth together.
He spoke of lilies, vines, and corn,
  The sparrow and the raven,
And words so natural, yet so wise,
  Were on men's hearts engraven;
And yeast, and bread, and flax, and cloth,
  And eggs, and fish, and candles;
See how the whole familiar world
  He most divinely handles.

T. T. LYNCH

❖❖❖

BEAUTIES OF NATURE

Nature has beauties which seem to have been fashioned for the sake of the sheer gladness they cause, and for no other reason.

The flower draws the bee with its scent or its color; but what of its graceful form, whose charm only the human mind can feel?

Why that purple glory of the mountain, with its nameless charm and power over the soul?

What use is there in the beauty of the rainbow's prism or of its perfect curve, or of the quivering leaflet at springtime, or of the midnight sky sown with stars?

The appreciation of the beautiful, whether in nature or in art, is the free gift of God, bestowed upon men out of His overflowing love.

They have been endowed with it, not merely in order that they may live, but more importantly in order that they may live happily.

Well, then, might the Prophets and Psalmists of olden days "sing of the loving-kindness of the Lord"—a loving-kindness that was "mightily shewn" unto men—seeing that it fills the whole domain of life and floods it with a gratuitous joy.

MORRIS JOSEPH

❖❖❖

INFLUENCE

We become like that with which we live,
like that which we look upon,
read, and hear.
If we like beautiful things,
we become beautiful in our spirit.
Those who see to it
that only beautiful thoughts
are accepted as guests
in their homes and hearts
become beautiful through constant contact
with high and holy thinking.

WILLIAM L. STIDGER

THE PATH OF THE STARS

Down through the spheres that chant the
    Name of One
  Who is the Law of Beauty and of Light
He came, and as He came the waiting
    Night
  Shook with the gladness of a Day begun;
And as He came, He said: Thy Will be
    done
  On Earth; and all His vibrant Words
    were white
And glistering with silver, and their might
  Was of the glory of a rising sun.

Unto the stars sang out His living words
  White and with silver, and their rhythmic
    sound
Was as a mighty symphony unfurled;
  And back from out the stars like homing
    birds
They fell in love upon the sleeping ground
  And were forever in a wakened world.

THOMAS S. JONES, JR.

FOOTSTEPS OF GOD

In all the vast and minute, we see the
unambiguous footsteps of the God who
gives its luster to the insect's wing and
wheels His throne upon the rolling world.

WILLIAM COWPER

HEAVEN BREAKS THROUGH

Wonderful is the way in which beauty
breaks through. It breaks through not
only at a few highly organized points. It
breaks through almost everywhere.

Even the minutest things reveal it as
well as the sublimest things, like the stars.
Whatever one sees through the micro-
scope, a bit of mould for example, is
charged with beauty. Everything, from a
dew-drop to a mountain, is the bearer of
beauty.

And yet beauty has no function, no
utility.

Its value is intrinsic, not extrinsic.

It is its own excuse for being.

It greases no wheels, it bakes no pud-
dings.

It is a gift of sheer grace, a gratuitous
largess.

It must imply behind things a Spirit
that enjoys beauty for its own sake and
that floods the world everywhere with it.

Wherever it can break through it does
break through, and our joy in it shows
that we are in some sense kindred to the
Giver and Revealer of it.

RUFUS M. JONES

TRUE BEAUTY

Christ came to reveal the gifts of God's
love which would restore the inner perspective of man, the quality and dimen-
sion of the lovely in our lives. True beauty
is where God's Spirit meets a life and
where that life responds like a frail flower
to the sun. When this "beauty of the Lord
our God" is upon us, then the splendor of
love, the colors of righteousness, and the
glory of brotherhood blend with the
beauty of earth and sky and sea.

SAMUEL J. SCHMIECHEN

MIRACLE

We muse on miracles who look
   But lightly on a rose!
Who gives it fragrance or the glint
   Of glory that it shows?

Who holds it here between the sky
   And earth's rain-softened sod?
The miracle of one pale rose
   Is proof enough of God!

EDITH DALEY

❖❖❖

NOT BY BREAD ALONE

Man does not live by bread alone, but by beauty and harmony, truth and goodness, work and recreation, affection and friendship, aspiration and worship.

Man does not live by bread alone, but by the splendor of the starry firmament at midnight, the glory of the heavens at dawn, the gorgeous blending of colors at sunset, the luxuriant loveliness of magnolia trees, the sheer magnificence of mountains.

Man does not live by bread alone, but by the majesty of ocean breakers, the shimmer of moonlight on a calm lake, the flashing silver of a mountain torrent, the exquisite patterns of snow crystals, the exalted creations of artists.

Man does not live by bread alone, but by the sweet song of the mockingbird, the rustle of tall corn in the breeze, the magic of the maestro's violin, the grandeur of Handel's *Messiah*, the sublimity of Beethoven's *Fifth Symphony*.

Man does not live by bread alone, but by the fragrance of roses, the scent of orange blossoms, the smell of new-mown hay, the clasp of a friend's hand, the tenderness of a mother's kiss.

Man does not live by bread alone, but by the lyrics and sonnets of poets, the mature wisdom of sages, the holiness of saints, the biographies of great souls.

Man does not live by bread alone, but by comradeship and high adventure, seeking and finding, creating and cooperating, serving and sharing, loving and being loved.

KIRBY PAGE

❖❖❖

On that first day new Adam saw the world,
It must have looked like this: sky, tree, and
   sod
Divinely beautiful and crystal clean,
Fresh from the hands of God.

This shining hour, when beauty gleams so
   bright
Earth seems to wear a golden aureole,
I share the joy of that first moment man
Became a living soul.

GAIL BROOK BURKET

❖❖❖

MIRACLES

Not believe in miracles, you say?
I witnessed many of them today!
The sunrise, from a clear calm sea at dawn,
Some golden dandelions nestling in the
   lawn,
A lacy cobweb swaying in the breeze,
Fragrant apple blossoms on such gnarly
   trees,
The melody of robins in the rain,
A mother's lullaby with soft refrain,
A tiny baby's smile, so pure and sweet,
Wee clinging fingers and pink dimpled
   feet,
The blazing glory of a sunset sky,
A soul released from pain, when death
   seemed nigh,
The tranquil ripple on the waving wheat,
The hush of evening on a village street,
The whispering murmur of cathedral
   pines—
To all these miracles, my humble heart
   resigns.

FRANCES E. WALKER

❖❖❖

INNER BEAUTY

There is little said in the Bible that would give us a clue as to Jesus' appearance. We know nothing about His height or weight. The color of His eyes, hair, and complexion we can only guess.

We do know that men, women, and children were attracted to Him singly and in multitudes, but His attraction was evidently not in His unmentioned physical appearance but in His compassion, His love, His forgiveness, and His gracious words.

People came to Him because of an inner beauty that the discerning were quick to find and appreciate.

One little girl once pensively said to her mother, "Mom, do you know, I think Jesus was the only one who dared to live His life inside out!"

His hidden beauty did not remain hidden.

HAROLD E. KOHN

❖❖❖

There is no beautifier of complexion, or form, or behavior, like the wish to scatter joy and not pain around us.

RALPH WALDO EMERSON

❖❖❖

THE WHITE FIRE OF BEAUTY

The pure white fire of beauty burns
   forever.
Cities may be blasted from the earth
And the cherished homes of men be felled;
   but never
Can loveliness be lost. The gentle mirth
Of wind goes rippling through the tawny
   grasses,
New flowers blossom from the latter rains;
All that is tortuous and ugly passes,
But beauty—beauty remains.

Life's troubled waters cannot quench that
   fire.
Men's hate can never blur the sun's gold
   light,
Nor mar the moon's pale silver, as still
   higher
The steadfast stars climb up earth's darkest
   night;
And love, love crushed within the hearts
   of men,
Will rise—will rise again!

GRACE NOLL CROWELL

❖❖❖

From THE PRAYER OF AGASSIZ

On the isle of Penikese,
Ringed about by sapphire seas,
Fanned by breezes salt and cool,
Stood the Master with his school . . .
Said the Master to the youth:
"We have come in search of truth,
Trying with uncertain key
Door by door of mystery . . .
We are groping here to find
What the hieroglyphics mean
Of the Unseen in the seen."

JOHN GREENLEAF WHITTIER

❖❖❖

GOD'S BOUNTY

Dawn plays no favorites. It paints
The canyons for us all. A stream
Is not exclusive. Touched by sun,
Its necklaces of diamonds gleam
For rich and poor. A poppy field
Is gold that can't be measured—free
To any passerby—and pines
That sing a mountain melody
Are everybody's trees. When dusk
Drops curtains on the waiting hills,
All feel its quiet curtains. Birds
Emit their sleepy evening trills
For all to hear. God bids us share
His bounty scattered everywhere!

MARIE DAERR

❖❖❖

PRAYER

Father of life, awake in me
    the joy of living in this day,
    all new in challenge and in hope.
O Lord of Love, lift up my heart
    amid the fathomless beauty of creation
    above all malice or apathy.
O living Christ, who died for me,
    fill up these precious hours
    with Thy redeeming radiance.
O God most high, may courage master me
    and banish fear.
Let gratitude repay Thy grace in glory
    unto Thee.

WILLIAM ROBERT MILLER

❖❖❖

WHO WALKS WITH SOUL AWAKE

Who walks the world with soul awake
    Finds beauty everywhere;
Though labor be his portion,
    Though sorrow be his share,
He looks beyond obscuring clouds,
    Sure that the light is there!

And if—the ills of mortal life
    Grown heavier to bear—
Doubt come with its perplexities
    And whisper of despair,
He turns with love to suffering men—
    And, lo! God, too, is there.

FLORENCE EARLE COATES

❖❖❖

WHAT IS BEAUTY TO YOU?

Beauty means this to one person, perhaps, and that to the other. And yet when any one of us has seen or heard or read that which to him is beautiful, he has known an emotion which is in every case the same in kind, if not in degree—an emotion precious and uplifting.

A choir boy's voice, a ship in sail, an opening flower, a town at night, the song of the blackbird, a lovely poem, leaf shadows, a child's grace, the starry skies, a cathedral, apple trees in spring, a thoroughbred horse, sheepbells on a hill, a rippling stream, a butterfly, the crescent moon—the thousand sights or sounds or words that evoke in us the thought of beauty—these are the drops of rain that keep the human spirit from death by drought. They are a soothing and a silent refreshment that we perhaps do not think about but which goes on all the time.

It would surprise any of us if we realized how much store we unconsciously set by beauty, and how little savor there would be left in life if it were withdrawn. It is the smile on the earth's face, open to all, and needs but eyes to see, the mood to understand.

JOHN GALSWORTHY

❖❖❖

REFLECTIONS

The external world reflects the mentality of the observer. Look at it with jaundiced eyes, and it gives back the yellow tinge of misery. Smile at it with clear vision, and it invites you into its rose gardens and sunshine.

F. A. HORNIBROOK

❖❖❖

PRAYER

We bring our broken lives to Thee
and pray Thee,
O Divine Musician,
win from us some mighty strain,
tune us to the harmony of Thy will,
make all our lives
a hymn of praise.

WILLIAM E. ORCHARD

❖❖❖

Climb the mountains and get their good tidings.

JOHN MUIR

❖❖❖

SING FORTH HIS PRAISE

How can our tongues keep silence when God's love
Shines out from every beauty we behold?
The stars that tell His glory from above
Declare His ways of wisdom from of old.

The morning light breaks forth in golden gleams
To speak the great Creator's power and might.
The sunlight sparkling on the field and streams
Reflects His kindly smiles of peace and light.

Each blossom of the woodland shows His care;
The mountain heights rejoice to praise His name.
The goodness of the Lord is everywhere.
The winds, and trees, and clouds spread forth His fame.

When earth and sky do not keep silent tongue,
But praise the sovereign God that gave them birth,
Should not His praises by our hearts be sung
And published to the ends of all the earth?

MARK BULLOCK

❖❖❖

Beauty is a poem for every heart to know.

HELEN MARING

216

EPILOGUE

✦✦✦

In the cathedral of Hereford, England, there hangs a map, one of the very few medieval maps we possess, and in the very center of this map is marked the city of Jerusalem.

Indeed, in Jerusalem itself, in the middle of the Church of the Holy Sepulchre, tourists are shown the point which medieval geographers believed to be the exact center of the world.

Visitors to either church usually smile when they are shown these things, and perhaps comment on the quaint simplicity of those former Christians who were so deluded, and even so conceited, as to hold such beliefs.

Today we are coming to understand that there was more wisdom in their simplicity than we should have admitted thirty years ago.

Christian historians are tending more and more to see the events of Christ's life as being in a very real sense the "center" of history, the crisis to which all previous history had looked, and without which no subsequent history can satisfactorily be explained.

It was the point at which God Himself entered the arena and acted directly upon history, the only point where it is possible to see visibly and concretely the eternal God at work in His temporal creation.

It was no accident that the climax of this critical life took place at Passover, since the Incarnation, the Crucifixion, and the Resurrection of Jesus are for the world what the Passover had been for the Jewish people—the great deliverance.

DENIS BALY

ACKNOWLEDGMENTS (*continued*)

Acknowledgment is made to the following estates for permission to reprint copyrighted material:

Estate of Leslie Savage Clark for "Beacon Light," "Carpenter," "Country Well Curb," "The Hands of Christ," "Master Builder," "The Pharisee," "Remembrance," and "Son of Man"; estate of Thomas Curtis Clark for "Amos, the Prophet of Justice," "By an Ancient Sea," "Moses," and "The Touch of Human Hands"; estate of Helen Frazee-Bower for "I Hold the Book" and "The Stranger"; estate of Marion Franklin Ham for "A Prayer"; estate of Merlo Heicher for "A Pilgrim in Palestine"; estate of Harry Kemp for "The Going of His Feet" and "Joses, the Brother of Jesus"; estate of Alice Meynell for "Easter Night"; estate of Ida Norton Munson for "The Open Door," "Pilate Washed His Hands," "The Road to Emmaus," "Sight," and "The Upper Room"; estate of William Alexander Percy for "His Peace" and "The Holy Women"; estate of Paul Scherer for quotation; estate of Harry B. Schultheis for quotation from *Christianity Today;* estate of Samuel M. Shoemaker for quotation; estate of Charles Hanson Towne for "The Deathless Tale."

Acknowledgment is made to the following persons for permission to reprint their copyrighted material as indicated:

Margaret E. Bruner for "Joseph of Arimathaea" from *Midstream;* Mark Bullock for "Sing Forth His Praise" from *Signs of the Times;* Gail Brook Burket for "The Doors of Heaven," "His Own," and "Shared Joy"; Aline Badger Carter for "Immortal Words"; Manfred A. Carter for "Words on the Wind"; Stanton A. Coblentz for "The Ancient Quest" and "As Sometimes, in a Tale"; Kendig Brubaker Cully for "One Light, One Love"; Marie Daerr for "God's Bounty"; Sara Henderson Hay for "After the Crucifixion"; Roy Helton for "Miracles"; Victoria Saffelle Johnson for "Dedication"; Edwin O. Kennedy for "The Carpenter's Son" and "The Friendly Universe"; Della Adams Leitner for "Open Thou Mine Eyes"; Earl Marlatt for "Crucifixion" and "Paul"; Madeleine Sweeny Miller for "The Bethlehem of Boaz" and "How Far to Bethlehem?"; Terence Y. Mullins for "On the Apostle's Creed" from *Christianity Today;* Marian Paust for "Christmas Prayer" in *P.E.O. Record;* Edith Lovejoy Pierce for "Communion" from *The Churchman* and "Jesus Wrote with His Finger on the Ground" and "May Peter's Choice Be Ours" from *Christian Century;* Johnstone G. Patrick for "Ecce Homo," "The Healer," "A Loaf of Bread, a Jug of Wine, and a Towel," and "Mary Magdalene" from *Above the Thorn,* "God and Man" from *Christian Century,* "Christmas Gifts" from *The Pulpit,* and "Nazareth"; Beatrice Plumb for "My Lord of Little Boats"; Ralph W. Seager for "Before the Ten Commandments," "Geography of Jesus," and "Sumac Is a Burning Bush"; Violet Alleyn Storey for "Little Prayer in April" from *A Poet Prays,* "After Calvary" and "A Country Church"; Hildegarde Hoyt Swift for "The Man of Galilee" and "The Teacher"; Gilbert Thomas for "Toward Jerusalem" from *Selected Poems;* Joan Truitt for "Lot's Wife" from *Presbyterian Life;* Ruth B. Van Deusen for "God Must Have Known"; Franklin Zahn for "Covenants and Recompense."

Acknowledgment is made to the following persons for permission to reprint from their writings:

Charles L. Allen, Marion C. Allen, A. Purnell Bailey, Walter Russell Bowie, Margueritte Harmon Bro, Robert W. Burns, William R. Cannon, Truman B. Douglass, Albert Edward Day, Nels F. S. Ferré, Harry Emerson Fosdick, Richard C. Halverson, Leonard Hodgson, David Lawrence, Gerhard E. Lenski, Mary Ely Lyman, John McDowell, John A. Mackay, Stephen Neill, Charles Schulz, Fulton J. Sheen, Elton Trueblood, Howard Thurman, Leslie D. Weatherhead.

INDEX OF PHOTOGRAPHS

Cover design by Amy Isbey

INDEX OF CONTRIBUTORS

INDEX OF POETRY

INDEX OF TOPICS